Love Is Not Enough

Breaking the Patterns That Break Your Relationships

For my mother — everything I know about love, I learned from losing you.
For my dad — who chose and loved me without strings attached.

*For my daughter — I can't protect you from a broken heart. What I can do is
make sure you're never without the tools to heal it. Most people were never taught
what you already know: how to build healthy relationships. Go practice.*

*And for every client who sat across from me and asked why — You were never
broken. You were just never taught.*

Contents

Introduction

You loved them. With all your heart. And it still fell apart.

Or maybe it hasn't fallen apart yet, but you can feel it happening, that slow, quiet unraveling that you cannot quite name and cannot quite stop, even though you are trying. Even though you have always been trying.

This is the part nobody talks about. Not really. We talk about communication. We talk about compatibility. We talk about love languages and attachment styles and red flags and green flags and every other piece of relationship vocabulary the internet has handed us in the last decade. But underneath all of it, underneath every framework and every quiz and every therapist's office and every late-night conversation with a friend who loves you but does not know what to tell you, there is a truth that most of us have lived but very few of us have been willing to say out loud.

Love is not enough.

It was not enough for Callie and Ryan, who were genuinely attached to each other and genuinely traumatized by each other in equal measure. It was not enough for Ashley and Jose, who desired each other completely and deceived each other completely at the same time. It was not enough for me, at nineteen years old, standing in a marriage I had walked into with real love and zero tools, wondering why something that felt so right kept going so wrong.

Love is real. I am not here to tell you it isn't. I have felt it. I have studied it. I have watched it change people's lives and I have watched it, on its own, without the right foundation beneath it, quietly destroy them. Love is real and love is necessary and love, by itself, is not enough.

So what is?

That is the question this book is designed to answer. Not in theory. In practice. With the science that explains what your brain is actually doing when you fall for someone, with the research that proves we were never explicitly taught how to do any of this, and with the honest, sometimes uncomfortable examination of the patterns we carry into every relationship we have ever been in, patterns we did not choose, patterns that were built into us long before we were old enough to know what a relationship was supposed to look like.

I did not set out to become a relationship expert. I set out to understand why love hurts. Every failed relationship I lived through, every client who sat across from me asking why, each one pushed me to study harder, listen more carefully, and find language for what most of us feel but cannot explain. And what I found, after years of research and working with clients and more personal trial and error than I care to fully recount, is this: the problem is almost never love. The problem is everything we bring to love that we were never taught to examine.

We absorb what we see. We internalize what we are shown. We mistake what is familiar for what is right. And then we go out into the world and build relationships from those inherited blueprints, wondering why they keep falling apart in the same places, with different people wearing different faces.

I went to the streets of New York City and asked over a thousand strangers three questions about relationships. The most startling thing I found was not what people said. It was what they couldn't say. No one I spoke to, not one person across every age, race, gender, and relationship status I encountered over five days in one of the most diverse cities on earth, could tell me they had been explicitly taught how to have a healthy relationship. Not one.

We learn about relationships the way we learn about everything else in the early years of our lives: by watching, by absorbing, by internalizing what the people around us model, whether those models are healthy or broken or somewhere in the complicated gray space between. And because most of the relationships we grow up watching are neither fully healthy nor fully broken, we arrive at adulthood with a distorted, incomplete, and often deeply flawed understanding of what love is supposed to look like and what it is supposed to feel like and what it is supposed to require from us.

Then we fall in love, and we are shocked when it is hard.

The Four Convictions

This book is not a communication guide. There are thousands of those and you do not need another one.

This book is a framework. A complete delivery of the Re/Model Framework™. Not an introduction to it. Not a sample of it. All of it. Specifically, it is the framework I wish someone had handed me at nineteen years old before I walked into a marriage I was not remotely equipped to sustain, and the framework I have spent the better part of two decades building, testing, and refining with the clients who have sat across from me in sessions and the audiences who have shown up to my events carrying the same questions in different languages.

The framework is built on four convictions that I will ask you to sit with as you read.

The first conviction is that you were not taught how to have a healthy relationship, and this is not your fault. It is, however, your responsibility to address.

The second conviction is that the patterns sabotaging your relationships right now were built before you were old enough to choose them, built in the households and the relationships and the cultural environments that shaped you, and that understanding where they came from is the first and most essential step toward changing them.

The third conviction is that love, real and genuine and deeply felt love, is not the foundation of a lasting relationship. It is the fuel. The foundation is something you have to build consciously, deliberately, and with full knowledge of what you are bringing to it.

The fourth conviction is that it is possible to build it. I have seen it done. I have helped people do it who came to me convinced they were too broken to try again. You are not too broken. But you may be operating from a blueprint that was never designed to build what you actually want.

Here is how the book is structured and why.

Section I, *How Did We Get Here*, is the diagnostic section. Before we can change the patterns, we have to see them clearly. These chapters examine where our relationship beliefs come from, how the family dynamics we grew up in became the silent curriculum we are still following, how cultural shifts have redefined what relationships are supposed to look like, how love works in the brain and why chemistry is not the same as compatibility, and what social media is doing to our ability to see our own relationships clearly.

Section II, *Breaking the Pattern*, is where we name the specific mechanisms of damage. It's also the beginning of Phase 1 of the framework: *Remove the Gridlock*. It asks you to do the hardest thing first: find the pattern. Name it. Trace it to the wound underneath it. Understand the ego that runs it and the mask that hides it. You cannot build anything real on top of a pattern you have not yet seen. Gridlock is what happens when the pattern runs unchecked. Removal is what happens when you finally decide to look at it directly.

Section III, *Recalibrate*, is where we rebuild. It's Phase 2 of the framework: *Recalibrate the Connection*. It does exactly what it sounds like. Not repair for its own sake. Not communication strategies layered over an unexamined foundation. Recalibration. The friendship that has to exist before romantic love can hold. The language of conflict that moves toward truth instead of away from it. The intimacy that has to be rebuilt rather than rekindled.

Section IV, *Begin Again*, is Phase 3 of the framework: *Accelerate the Results*. This is where we face the hardest part: loss. breakups, grief, the neuropsychology of what happens to your brain when an attachment ends. Acceleration does not mean speed. It means depth. Moving through loss completely enough that what you build next is built on something real. Stepping back into love not with the same blueprint but with a new one. One you built on purpose. That is what the Re/Model Framework delivers.

A few things I need to ask of you before we go further.

I need you to be willing to be honest with yourself. Not with me. I am not in the room. But with yourself, about the patterns you recognize, the behaviors you have justified, the beliefs you have inherited and never questioned. This book will ask you to look at some things that are uncomfortable. I am asking you to look anyway.

I need you to be willing to dispel what you think you already know. So often we are shaped by what is in our small group, our family, our friends, our limited media intake, and we believe we have a pretty good worldview on these issues. We do not. I want you to be free of those limitations so you will be open to the realities and the possibilities I am going to lay out for you here.

And I need you to understand, before you read another word, that nothing in this book is an indictment of who you are. It is an examination of what you were taught. There is a difference, and that difference is everything.

You are not broken. You are patterned. And patterns, unlike character, can be changed.

Before you go any further, I want you to do something.

Go to the link below and take the Re/Model Pattern Assessment. It takes about three minutes. It will identify your dominant relationship pattern, name the specific fears driving it, and give you a clear picture of how it is showing up in your relationships right now. The self-awareness you bring into this book will determine how much of it actually lands.

Take it now, before Chapter 1. Come back and keep reading.

Everything starts here.

**Re/Model Pattern Assessment at www.carloshines.com/quiz
or scan the QR Code below**

I

How Did We Get Here

We learn how to have relationships in general through the implicit attitudes and behaviors of those around us, but we don't necessarily learn how to have healthy relationships.

Who Taught You That?

Through no fault of my own, I was damaged goods.

Medically speaking, I am not supposed to be here. When my mother had her last child, or the child she'd believed was her last at age twenty-eight, she underwent a tubal ligation afterward. Believing she was free and clear of the worry and the ability to have more children, you can imagine her surprise when she found she was pregnant once again. This time, with me.

But conversely, I was destined to be here. A man releases 100 million sperm cells each time he ejaculates. These millions of sperm cells compete with one another to fertilize an egg in a process called sperm competition. A vast majority of those die off in the vaginal canal because they're too weak or have some sort of structural or genetic defect. I like to think that the sperm containing me was a hardcore, motivated, badass fighter, because it defied the stacked odds and flourished in an environment designed to reject it.

My inconceivable beginnings serve as a bit of a metaphor for the feelings of otherness and confusion that clouded most of my childhood. I don't think my story is one of beating the odds, but is rather a story of facing them and learning from them. In the second grade, I was diagnosed with Dyslexia. By the time I reached third grade, I was in a special education class with fifteen other students. The other students and I were much different from each other. All fifteen of us were unique, idiomatic individuals, and our personalities didn't always mesh, so to speak. Our interactions were, at times, very rocky and cold.

Special Education instilled in me the value of not judging a book by its cover. After all, at the time, I wouldn't have wanted someone to judge me by mine. I learned then that people often see the world from a very narrow perspective. There is no such thing as good or bad, black or white. There is, however, the gray in between, and I'm continually reminded of this fact. Relationships: family, friends, and romantic ones are full of gray matter. They play a crucial role in allowing us to function normally day to day.

From this, I learned empathy: the ability to see beyond appearances and connect with others' experiences, recognizing the depth and complexity in each individual.

Inheritance of Dysfunction

Each person in my family became a teacher in the unspoken classroom of relationships. They laid the groundwork for the relationships I'd engage in later in life, but were quite complicated in and of themselves. My mom became an angel far too early. I was just fourteen years old. When she passed, the house went cold and silent. The air felt different: still, heavy, and too aware of itself. I remember staring at her favorite red leather chair for weeks, expecting it to move, knowing in my heart without proof that the normalcy of my life as I had known it died with her.

Growing up, we lived with my brothers, who were much older than I, and none of them wanted much to do with me at all. Not because they had anything against me, but because they perceived their lives to be more important than mine, or those of anyone else around them, for that matter. As a result, I didn't know my brothers. We lived together, but I can't recall a time when they took me to a park to play, to a restaurant for breakfast, or even to eat a meal with them at the dinner table. In my own home, I felt invisible and ignored. When our mother became sick, they left me to care for her. How could I, still just a child, manage such a large, glaring responsibility while they went about minding their own, self-centered business? This is a question I still cannot answer. I loved my brothers, but they placed a responsibility on me that was too heavy to bear. It wasn't until I was older and gained a bit of perspective that I understood.

From my brothers, I learned distrust: a hesitance to rely on others, rooted in the early realization that even family can let you down. I didn't have words for it then, but distrust became a kind of armor. I wore it everywhere. Even around people who meant well.

But while my brothers familiarized me with the idea of low self-confidence and notions of loneliness, my mother sought to do the opposite. Throughout my childhood, she instilled in me the value of love and kindness. My socialization experience was affected by her subconscious teachings: how to love, how to care for others, and how to be mindful of others' needs. I was different than other male children, and my mother knew this. She reminded me to ignore the negative voices of those around me and, in the absence of their noise, she encouraged me to live freely, unapologetically, and authentically. She'd made mistakes raising my older brothers, and she was honest about that. She wanted to raise me differently and poured every ounce of her love, attention, and personality into me. My relationship with my mother was short-lived yet loving and healthy, and for that, I'm grateful.

From this, I learned self-worth: the understanding that I deserved love, acceptance, and the freedom to be myself, no matter what others thought.

I knew who my biological father was, but he had long decided he wanted nothing to do with me. I was his illegitimate child, conceived while he was cheating on his wife. I longed for a relationship with him. I felt empty on the inside because of not having him around. I was in a constant state of wanting someone who didn't want me. I burned with the desire to have a relationship with him, but he rejected me. Rejection is a trauma that whispers you're unworthy. I didn't let this desire, nor his rejection, destroy me. At least, that's what I'd believed. As a young adult, I began to see the effects of his rejection through the lens of abandonment. I was afraid of getting close to people, with the fear that they too would leave.

From this, I learned guardedness: a protective instinct to keep people at arm's length, fearing that closeness would only lead to hurt and abandonment.

I was adopted later in my childhood. The man I call my dad, my adopted father, taught me the power of love. My mother knew the man who would adopt me after her demise. He was a minister at the church we attended.

Although the official adoption did not become finalized until I was sixteen years old, he was my sanity while going through turbulence with my actual family. He pushed me to reach my full potential and prioritized teaching me everything he knew. I was his first and only son. He loved me without expectations, but, in a way, I learned the ins and outs of those expectations, controlling them to my advantage. He had an authoritarian parenting approach, which I subconsciously emulated and internalized, and which led to the development of my own controlling tendencies. He rejected toxic masculinity and taught me how to set boundaries, embrace my emotions, and express myself.

My dad is an expert communicator, and in turn, taught me the value of communicating openly, regardless of my smart mouth and unrelenting sarcasm. Because of my feelings of worthlessness, I would often ask him, "Why me?" He'd recite 1 Corinthians 13, and I internalized the Bible's definition of love. My dad embodies the essence of that scripture. He made me feel valued, wanted, seen, and respected, and I hold an immeasurable amount of love and gratitude toward him that cannot be expressed in words. Most poignantly, as I write this, the thought of my dad's love causes tears of gratitude, appreciation, and emotion to stream down my face.

From this, I learned unconditional love: the profound impact of being seen, valued, and supported without strings attached, which became the foundation of my self-worth and my understanding of true connection.

My extended family similarly played a formative role in my socialization experience. My mother and her sisters were very close. Conflict was ripe in their relationships, and their large, vivacious personalities often sought control and dominance over each other's similarly big personas. Their personality clashes played a paramount part in the success and failure of their relationships, and oftentimes, my mother and her sisters would fight about things I found silly. When they did fight, they wouldn't speak to the other sister for weeks or months and would gossip about the "out" sister. Unfortunately, there were occasions where the "out" sister would take her anger out on the other sisters' children and would not allow the cousins to see each other.

However, even when times were bad, horrible even, the sisters were still there for one another in some capacity. Relationships should be communal, not transactional, but I do not think they had the language to understand this at the time. Years of watching their quarrels and troubles offered me something I never thought I'd give them credit for: an anthropological history lesson in relationship dynamics.

I had a virtually nonexistent relationship with my older cousins. Those relationships felt much like the ones I had with my brothers. On the other hand, my relationship with my younger cousins, who were around my age, was more involved. We spent time together often and were friends before cousins. Our conversations were about more than life updates. I felt truly emotionally connected with them, and we communicated often. We fought, don't get me wrong, and we fought often. At times, I covered for my cousins and took ass-whoopings for them so they wouldn't get in trouble, and vice versa. But we fought like we loved: fairly and honestly. We'd get together and scheme, devising plans to get what we wanted from our parents, like ice cream from the truck or more time outside before the streetlights turned off. But amid this scheming grew cooperation and communication. I loved my cousins, and they loved me. As we grew older, life and its happenings got in the way of our relationship. We all went our separate ways, and the bond we'd formed receded, eventually subsiding altogether.

From this, I learned the bittersweet reality that even the closest bonds can fade with time, as life naturally pulls people in different directions.

What They Called Me

I was eight years old the first time I was called a faggot. I wasn't a traditionally masculine child. I wanted to be a teacher and loved to read and write. My family noticed that, unlike my brothers and cousins, I preferred indoor activities and wasn't interested in traditionally "boy" things such as basketball and video games. Because of this, they called me a "homo" and a "faggot." But how could I, as a child, understand the traits of "men" when I didn't have a father figure until my early teens? In hindsight, I think I was exercising my early gender identity and bucking up against the system that taught me that, because of who I was, I was lesser than. I didn't want to be different or to stand out, but deep down, I knew I didn't quite fit in with my family.

My adult relatives called me a faggot so often that, by thirteen, I began to believe them. Adults must be very careful with their external words because they quickly become a child's internal wounds. There's one incident sealed in my memory that I wish could be removed. An adult family member took me to their friend's house when I was fifteen or so and asked the adult friend to ascertain whether or not I was a "faggot." I overheard their conversation and heard the relative say, "Watch him. Look at how he moves his hands when he talks! And he doesn't like basketball! What boy do you know that doesn't like basketball, girl? What do you think?" To which the friend replied, "Yup. He's a faggot." I remember feeling my heart harden right then and there. I couldn't allow myself to exist in spaces where people tolerated me but did not accept me. I wanted nothing to do with those who sought to beat me down rather than lift me up. Wow. What a lesson to learn at such an early age.

From this, I learned alienation: the feeling of being pushed away by those who should have offered acceptance, leaving me to find my own path in a world that often felt unwelcoming.

Let me be clear. There isn't anything wrong with being gay. That wasn't the problem. I just wasn't. Today, those around me ask why I'm an LGBTQIA+ advocate, and my response is always the same: "People should be free to be themselves regardless of how others feel about it." The real reason, however, is because of my family. Their mislabeling, mistreatment, and misguided judgment produced my advocacy, to reject the notion of otherness and instead embrace inclusiveness.

Those stories are the experiences that shaped how I began to see relationships. Through the ups and downs, the trials and tribulations, and the heartaches, these family connections were my harshest instructors, unveiling the harsh reality of how they can deeply wound and scar us. As I look back on these painful lessons, it's a stark reminder that relationships can also be ruthless, leaving us emotionally battered and forever changed, often for the worse. But at the same time, I am reminded that despite the pain and challenges, relationships hold the power to transform us, to make us more resilient, compassionate, and ultimately, better versions of ourselves.

Undoubtedly, because of trauma, I have a unique ability to detach from others quite easily and never look back. Over time and with repeated, derogatory name-calling, I grew reclusive, no longer trusting those I was told to love. I felt as though everyone around me had a hidden agenda. I felt like a test subject in an experiment gone wrong, and this feeling permeated my adult life. Most importantly, I felt like being me was a mistake. Those who claim to love you are often, unfortunately, the ones to hurt you and make you feel less than enough. My family, though I do believe they loved me, mistreated me, and I grew up believing that this abuse was love. Their masked toxicity killed my ego, and I was effectively punished for being a little different. Can you imagine growing up thinking that abuse is love?

Nevertheless, the toxic masculinity I adopted became my downfall. During the years that followed, and well into my adulthood, I feebly tried to overcompensate for my natural inclinations and adopted a persona plagued by toxic masculinity and trauma.

Unconsciously and consciously, I wanted to prove that I wasn't what they'd labeled me, so I allowed my toxicity to run rampant. To prove my masculinity, I engaged in sexual activities with multiple women, simply to solidify my manliness. And somewhere deep down inside, I also think I was trying to prove this to myself. After all, I'd started to believe their words about me being gay.

The Blueprint is Wrong

Too often in our society, boys are taught that we must constantly prove our worth and masculinity, but there is never guidance on how or why. What we do, then, is utilize the extremes. We use our penises to substantiate our masculinity and use money to prove our worth. However, neither of these measures is truly indicative of what it means to be a respectable and dignified man. Society is ultimately comfortable with men feeling less than, so long as they provide or give something to their partners or families.

As a researcher, I've come to realize that this is the problem with men today. Due to societal expectations and misconceptions, modern men are experiencing higher levels of loneliness and suicide compared to previous generations. Modern men, largely, are far less likely to be interested in marriage. They are opting out because they do not see it as a desirable or rewarding option in the current social and legal climate. They no longer want to subscribe to the belief that they will be loved only if they can provide, because they are deserving of love regardless of their ability to do so. Their being worthy of love must not come with strings attached. Full stop.

Married to Early

At nineteen, I got married. I did it for two reasons. Firstly, I married her because I loved her, or so I thought. Secondly, I married her to rebel against my father. I wanted to show him that finally, I was in control of my life, and for the first time, he couldn't do anything to stop me. My past traumas haunted me in my marriage. Everything that was wrong on the inside came to light. Relationships have a funny way of revealing our flaws. Sometimes, I was an expert communicator, but often it arose in the form of long, torrid, hysterical arguments filled with criticism covered in sarcasm. Up to that point, except for my dad, everyone had hurt me in some way or another. Part of me was expecting her to do the same. I preempted her leaving, pushing her away so I could see it coming. Little did I know, she loved every broken part of me, and she didn't leave. I had no idea what was going on with me, nor the reasons why my marriage wasn't working. We just kept pointing fingers at one another. We were too young to be married and too silly to understand the weight of the responsibility that came with it.

The issues were numerous. I was not entirely ready for marriage or any kind of serious relationship, for that matter. I went into marriage as a child of only single-parent households and had little bearing or idea as to what a two-parent arrangement might look like, nor did I have the tools necessary to maintain a healthy marriage. Because I was married as a teenager, I didn't yet know who I was as a person. Unknowingly, I brought all my past traumas, failures, doubts, and my inflated ego into my marriage. The doubt I'd learned as a child caused jealousy within our relationship, and my residual low self-esteem required me to constantly seek validation from my partner. Following the years I'd spent learning the act of betrayal, I was in search of trust and began to question her loyalty, requiring her to prove it to me consistently. Into my marriage, I brought the controlling mannerisms I'd learned from my father and lacked the ability to negotiate and compromise, which were my ex-wife's greatest strengths. At the time, being blinded by my trauma, I simply couldn't see it.

Sex was the only thing in our marriage that did work. We knew how to be intimate with one another, and sex became what we believed was the solution to our issues. We'd argue and give one another the silent treatment for days, but one thing was certain: even in our anger, even amid the silent treatment, we used sex to escape. I know what you're thinking. No, we didn't kiss and make up after sex. Instead, we went right back to anger and the silent treatment. Somehow, during her childhood, she'd learned that sex would make things better, and that if you gave it to a man, he'd forget what might be wrong. It was her default, and as great as the sex was, it didn't fix anything.

When things took a turn for the worse and I began pushing away, we tried to fix things spiritually. We prayed together and conducted Bible study at home. We believed that God would fix the areas of our relationship that were undoubtedly broken, because that's what we'd been taught in church. But, over time, we began to realize that this too wasn't working. Now, I understand why. Christianity taught us that God would fix all of our problems if we just pray and wait on Him. But we needed more than prayer. The scripture states, "Faith without works is dead." We needed therapy, tools to help us navigate our marriage as teenagers, a support system we didn't have, and a commitment to do the work needed to save our relationship. The marriage lasted five years because, at the first sign of betrayal, which wasn't betrayal, but I'd perceived it as such, I gave up on us. But this too was confounding. I didn't give up. The traumatized child in me did. As I said previously, I can disconnect and walk away, and that trait proved incredibly detrimental.

All of this hurt my marriage, as well as the several relationships that followed, until I decided enough was enough. I went to therapy and, sitting in front of the therapist with tears rolling down my face, I begged her to help heal me. I felt I was too damaged and too broken to be in a relationship. The relationships I engaged in kept falling apart around me because I knew I needed to be better. I had to face the monsters looming behind my closet door, monsters that were placed there by those responsible for raising me. A small community titled, "Family."

It wasn't until several years later that I began to understand why marriages fail. I enrolled in a graduate school class called Marriage and Family Dynamics. We were learning about various theoretical perspectives related to family dynamics and relationships, such as systems theory, attachment theory, and social learning theory, as well as relationship life cycles: the stages of relationships and the various challenges and transitions that families face as they progress through each stage.

During the class, I suddenly realized that other than my trauma and our ages as defining factors, our marriage ended because we were not cognizant of ourselves. We didn't know who we were as individuals, what we wanted, and furthermore, neither of us were validated as children. So, when we got married, we were looking for the validation we hadn't received from our parents in one another.

This habit is much more common than you might believe. We expect our partners to repeat the gifts and fill in the gaps our parents gave and left in us. **Stop.** Please go back and re-read the previous sentence because it is a common and often problematic assumption in relationships today. On one hand, it is natural for us to seek out partners who possess positive qualities or attributes reminiscent of our parents or other positive role models. But on the other hand, expecting a partner to fill the gaps that our parents left can be problematic, as it places unrealistic expectations and responsibilities on the relationship and on your partner. No singular person can fulfill all our needs and desires, and it is unfair to expect our partners to do so. If we are not aware of our own expectations and needs, we will end up projecting our unresolved issues onto our partners, which causes unnecessary conflict and tension in the relationship.

In my marriage, I was too young and immature to realize that the decisions I'd made would reverberate for years to come. Throughout my teens and well into my adult life, I didn't feel loved, and consequently, I never felt as though I was enough for anyone. Psychologists and sociologists alike can attest to the fact that we learn to love ourselves in the context of our relationships with others. I had great training for being miserable on the inside and smiling on the outside. I was a product of my upbringing, and a faulty one at that. I hurt others the way I learned to hurt them, and I felt guilty as a result. My guilt and past circled around each other like a clan of hungry hyenas excited to kill their prey, culminating in a cycle of toxicity, anguish, hurt, self-hate, and pain that only seemed to rinse and repeat.

Everything I brought into that marriage had a name I didn't know yet. The distrust I had learned from my brothers. The guardedness I had built around my father's absence. The controlling tendencies I had absorbed from my adopted father without realizing I was absorbing them. The desperate need for validation from someone who would finally stay. All of it had a name. I just hadn't found the language for it yet.

Yours have a name too. If you took the Re/Model Pattern Assessment before this Chapter, you already know what it is. If you haven't, stop here. Take it now. What you are about to read will land completely differently once you know what you are looking for.

Go to: www.carloshines.com/quiz or scan the QR Code at the end of the introduction. Then come back. Keep reading.

Relationships that Followed

In the next couple of relationships, I took on the role of protector and provider, believing it would make up for my failed marriage and reduce the impact of my guilty feelings laden with trauma. I am blessed that, in my family, I never witnessed any domestic violence situations. However, when I dated Haley, I learned the depth of what domestic violence can do to a child.

Growing up, Haley watched her parents fight often, and when they did, they fought physically. She learned that love comes with violence and believed the two to be virtually synonymous with each other. Haley believed that conflict and aggression were proof of love, and she operated from that belief inside our relationship every single day.

Her love language was chaos, and I didn't understand it. I was head over heels for Haley, and I would've done anything to make her happy. Growing up, the only advice I'd ever received about relationships was from my mother, who told me, "You only treat girls the way you want a man to treat me." Those words lived in me. I thought I'd built them into my foundation.

What I didn't understand then is that it doesn't matter how solid your foundation is if someone else's trauma keeps digging underneath it. The longer I stayed in that relationship, the more I noticed something shifting in me. Not all at once. Gradually. The way a person changes without realizing it until they catch themselves in the mirror one day and don't quite recognize who's looking back. I was becoming reactive in ways that weren't me. Thinking things I had no business thinking. Feeling pulled toward responses I had promised myself, and promised my mother, I would never entertain.

I left not because I stopped loving Haley. I left because I could see that I was becoming a person I was not willing to be.

I want you to sit with that for a second, because I want you to understand the full weight of what I'm telling you. This was not a situation where I lost my temper in a moment of passion. This was a situation where another person's trauma had reached inside of me and activated something I believed I did not have. That is how powerful unhealed pain is. Not just your own. Other people's too.

That relationship became my hardest teacher: love without boundaries turns into punishment for both people.

Despite how much another person needs you to love them in their way, if that way violates your morals or beliefs, you must walk away. Immediately. My relationship with Haley, by far, motivated me to learn about childhood attachment trauma and how our parents' parenting style influences our actions in romantic relationships.

The Questions That Changed Everything

My early family relationships are what inspired me to become a psychologist and to specialize in both Trauma and Marriage and Family Therapy. After years of observing my own family as a sort of case study, I maintained a deep yearning to learn more about family dynamics. At first, I just wanted to help others, but the more I learned and studied psychology, the more I realized I was truly looking for answers to questions I'd found burning inside me growing up. How can someone who says they love you hurt you so deeply? What happens afterward? How does this burning hurt manifest as we grow and form relationships of our own?

Every relationship in this chapter taught me something. I listed those lessons as I lived them. But here is what I understand now that I couldn't understand then: those lessons were not random. They were building something. Distrust and guardedness and the hunger for unconditional love and the terror of abandonment — those are not personality quirks. They are the raw materials that four very specific relational patterns are built from. The same patterns that are operating in your relationships right now. The pattern assessment will name which one is yours. The rest of this book will show you where it came from, what it has cost you, and what it is going to take to change it.

So let's go deeper.

The Hidden Curriculum

I spent a great deal of time investigating how we learn about relationships because it truly opens the gateway to understanding everything about their inner workings.

The Spark in Graduate School

I remember this vividly. I was in graduate school talking to a group of my peers about psychology and therapy, but more specifically, relationships. My peers seemed to brush off my concerns. In fact, one of them commented, "It's not that serious. The text and empirical articles give a good enough foundation." And yes, on the surface, that was true. But in my mind, I couldn't quite shake the feeling that there must be more to it.

I found myself questioning the very foundations of what I had been taught and searching for a deeper understanding of how to truly serve and make a life-changing impact on others. When I considered these questions, looking beyond textbooks, Google searches, academic articles, and interviews with professors and colleagues, I found both a wealth and a lack of knowledge.

The irony was a strange and perplexing realization. Not because there wasn't any research on the matter, but because the research was either too old, over two or three decades, or the studies monitored individuals throughout adolescence into young adulthood without controlling for external factors that play a large role in providing the answers I was looking for. In addition, most of the research was biased. The researchers primarily used white individuals, excluding people of color. Much of the research I stumbled upon was also limited to small geographical locations. I wanted to find research that included every race, gender, and culture to get an accurate, comprehensive result, one that reflects the diverse world we live in. So when I said I found a lot and nothing at the same time, this is what I meant.

I knew that if I was going to be the best at what I do, I needed unbiased and all-inclusive research. So to that end, I decided to do the research on my own.

Taking It to the Streets

I went to the streets of New York City, arguably the most diverse city in the United States. I spent five days in Midtown Manhattan and asked over a thousand strangers the following three questions:

1. Do you know any couples that inspire you? You cannot name celebrity couples.
2. Do you know of any couples who have been together for six or more years and still have that spark?
3. Were you specifically taught how to have healthy relationships, and if so, by whom?

I asked anyone who would talk to me: all genders, races, ethnicities, financial and socioeconomic backgrounds, and relationship statuses. I focused on those between the ages of sixteen and eighty-two because I needed a complete range of responses to fully understand the weight of my three questions across several generations.

I want to be upfront about something before I share what I found. This was not a controlled academic study. I am not presenting it as one. What I was doing was illustrative fieldwork, a qualitative snapshot of real people answering real questions on the street. I wasn't trying to publish in a journal. I was trying to understand what was happening out there, in actual human lives, beyond what the textbooks were telling me. And what I found stunned me.

What the Data Revealed

Only 20% of the people I spoke to said they knew of one or two couples who inspired them. Fourteen percent of those interviewed said the couples they knew who'd been together longer than six years had lost their spark or just didn't like each other anymore. Most shockingly, no one I talked to said they were taught how to have a healthy relationship. And I mean no one.

I was absolutely dumbfounded by the results. I'd believed that the hopes and assumptions that formed my hypothesis, that people are explicitly taught how to have healthy relationships by family members, would be accurate. My research proved otherwise.

Some of the people I interviewed brought me to tears. Their answers to the questions I asked provoked feelings of empathy for them and a deep sadness within me as I reflected on my own upbringing. Many of those I spoke with began to realize throughout our conversations why they might have unhealthy relationship patterns and, more importantly, why they'd found themselves in toxic relationships.

I truly believed that I was the outlier. It took me years of research and studying the DSM-5 to fully understand the complexity of my own family dynamic, which was highly dysfunctional, and how it affected the way I learned about relationships. I thought this hypothesis was generally true for most people, and simply didn't weave its way into my family's dinner table conversations. But the research proved that although we have vastly different phenotypes, we are all connected by a pedigree, one that raises an astounding alarm: many of us aren't explicitly taught about relationships. My hypothesis was wrong, but I was onto something big.

Here is what that finding means in terms of the patterns you carry.

The implicit beliefs that shape us, the socialization that conditions us, the direct experiences that wound us, the cultural norms that confine us, the media that distorts us — these are not five separate forces. They are five delivery systems for the same thing. The blueprint. The one that, long before you were old enough to choose it, decided how you would respond when love got close. Whether you would move toward it or away from it. Whether you would fight for it or test it or give yourself away in pursuit of it.

The pattern you identified in the assessment didn't arrive out of nowhere. It was built in exactly the ways this chapter describes.

The Hidden Curriculum of Relationships

We learn how to have relationships in general through the implicit attitudes and behaviors of those around us, but we don't necessarily learn how to have healthy relationships. My research proved this. It showed that people aren't taught explicitly about relationships, leaving us to unconsciously rely on what we see and hear as a kind of barometer for our adult relationships. That brings us to an outstanding yet paramount question, one that truly serves as a foundation for understanding why we do what we do, believe what we believe, and act the way we act about relationships.

Who taught you that?

It's a thought-provoking question without a straightforward answer, because we learn about relationships mostly by observing other relationships. Who taught you that doesn't provoke one definitive answer, but instead, many. Many of us learn how to have relationships through societal norms, direct experiences, and social media, but each of those comes with its own set of issues.

When we see relationships around us or in the media, we implicitly learn about trust, commitment, and communication dynamics. Most people learn about relationships through a combination of implicit beliefs, socialization, direct experiences, cultural norms, and what's presented in the media. Let's take a moment to discuss each of these a little deeper.

Implicit Beliefs impact the way we view and approach our own relationships. Implicit beliefs aren't conscious. We don't know they're there. They're the attitudes, beliefs, feelings, opinions, and behaviors we engage in and hold without conscious awareness. That's why we don't necessarily understand how, why, or where we learn to engage in relationships. Changing implicit beliefs is difficult because the process happens unconsciously, but it's possible to change it through willful recognition, hyper-awareness, and an eagerness to reset what we know.

One woman I spoke to in New York City said she didn't realize she equated arguing with passion until her partner stopped fighting back. "It felt empty," she told me, "like he didn't care anymore." That's an implicit belief operating in real time: conflict as proof of love.

Socialization is the process through which we learn the values, beliefs, and behaviors expected of us within our culture. It begins in childhood. As we see relationships in our households, surrounding family, and friends, we internalize what we witness. But it doesn't stop there. We continue this learning process throughout our entire lives.

Socialization influences our understanding of what's appropriate and what isn't within intimate relationships. A man in his forties told me he still believed men shouldn't cry because his father never did. "When my wife gets emotional, I freeze," he said. "It feels wrong to show it back." That's socialization: emotional restraint disguised as strength.

Direct Experiences are the personal interactions and relationships a person has with others and can be characterized as positive or negative. Experiences involve both what we see and where information is presented. Direct experiences involve not only romantic relationships but platonic ones as well. The relationships we're exposed to between friends and family members are often most formative and likely to play out in romantic relationships as well. We learn about trust, communication, commitment, and loyalty through our experiences with others.

If someone has supportive, caring, uplifting parents growing up, or a romantic partner who engages their interests and supports their future, they learn how to support others in a healthy way. If someone experiences a relationship with a communicative, direct, respectful partner, they learn how to communicate effectively too. Pretty simple.

On the other hand, if an individual either witnessed growing up or finds themselves in a pattern of negative experiences, like constant arguing, allowing disrespect, or abuse, either physical or emotional, they learn about the negative dynamics that occur in unhealthy relationships. Remember Haley? It's highly probable that they will mimic this dynamic in their current relationship and future ones. I'll go into more detail about relationship patterns in later chapters. For now, let's just focus on the basics.

When you step back, you can see how each of these layers: our beliefs, our upbringing, and our lived experiences, creates the silent syllabus of love. We follow its lessons instinctively, often without questioning who wrote them. Before looking at culture and media, pause and ask yourself: which lessons are still teaching you?

Cultural Norms play a role as well. Cultural norms involve the values, beliefs, and behaviors considered typical or acceptable in a certain culture. Norms shape our understanding of what is or isn't socially acceptable and influence how we interact with our romantic partners. If someone grows up in a region that values a traditional, nuclear family dynamic, they will adopt this model for themselves.

A couple I spoke to from the Bronx told me that their biggest challenge wasn't love but expectation. "Our families wanted us to play roles that didn't fit," they said. Cultural norms aren't just beliefs. They're scripts we inherit and struggle to rewrite.

The Media Mirage

That's not all. **Media**, including television, movies, music, and social media, which I argue is the single most negatively influential source of information on relationships, serves as a model for our behavior. It's important to note that media and how it presents relationships is not the healthiest way to learn positive relationship behaviors. Media presentations of relationships often perpetuate negative or even harmful ideas and stereotypes about what a relationship might look like.

Relationships in media are prone to distortion. Don't believe everything you see, especially online. After all, online relationships are deceptive. We see good times and glory, a split second of another person's life. We don't get to see what's happening when the camera is turned off. As a result, we fall in love with the idea of romantic dates, twinning, and crave a perfect relationship just like Blake Lively and Ryan Reynolds or Gabrielle Union and Dwyane Wade. We fall in love with the idea of love but lack the commitment to work hard to keep it. Media subconsciously teaches us that good and healthy relationships are about fun and games around the clock, when in reality, healthy relationships are fun AND hard work. We have this distorted idea that it shouldn't be hard. But don't let your idea of a relationship corrupt your reality of relationships.

I have a friend who loves the TV show Grey's Anatomy. We went to coffee once and started talking about the characters and relationships on the show. She's a Christina Yang and Miranda Bailey fan, by the way. We stumbled on the idea that many relationships in the show, including Meredith and Derek's, Lexie and Mark's, Owen and Christina's, all begin with sex. Not only that, but each relationship presented different, yet nevertheless stereotypical, ideas of gender roles. Meredith struggled to be both a mom and a surgeon. Owen pressured Christina to have kids when she didn't want to.

When I mentioned this, my friend's eyes widened as she took a large sip of her vanilla latte. I seized the opportunity to push a little further and said, "The show reeks of patriarchy, traditional gender roles, and serial monogamous sexual experiences wrapped up in a beautiful red bow that almost always leaves the women characters perplexed in their emotions, while the men enjoy the privileges of patriarchy, lacking the emotional language to be truthful about their feelings."

That pissed my friend off. She clapped back with, "Carlos, why can't you just watch a show and enjoy it without psychologizing its characters and ruining it for me? Now I won't be able to watch it without seeing that!" She quickly changed the subject.

This is just one example, but if you really think about it, many TV shows, social media platforms, and media outlets showcase relationships that come loaded with positive and negative expectations. When the media presents relationships filled with arguments, frequent breakups, infidelity, and drama, we think it's the norm and expect these dynamics in our own lives. We unconsciously act out these negative patterns, perpetuate unhealthy dynamics, and bond to a socialization experience that was never ours to adopt in the first place. One teenager told me she measures love by how much her boyfriend posts about her online. That's the new mirror: affection by algorithm.

Relearning What We Think We Know

In the long run, our lack of positive examples damages our ability to create and maintain successful and healthy romantic relationships. We aren't always exposed to positive role models, and it's difficult for us to understand what a healthy relationship looks like. At the end of the day, we begin to emulate these behaviors and patterns, leading to discontent and unhappiness. Unfortunately, many of us believe it's simply normal. I know I did. How about you?

Can we quickly discuss how a lack of positive relationship examples causes us to create unrealistic expectations? If you spend hours watching TikTok, Instagram, and YouTube couples or scrolling any social media platform, you might believe that relationships just shouldn't develop problems. You're wrong, but you're not alone. The fact of the matter is, they are perpetuating an illusion of perfection, but perfect relationships do not exist.

We see these social media couples and desire what they have, without realizing that we might start to believe that gifts, expensive trips, three-hundred-dollar steak dinners, and huge parties are the norm. Maybe you and your partner can't afford a trip, but you can afford to buy fake palm trees from Walmart, a picnic basket with food and utensils, drive down to the beach, and have a great time pretending you're on an island. Instead of being creative, we internalize other people's relationships, believe they're perfect, and in turn, look down on our own.

The truth is, most influencers and celebrities don't post about hardships and conflict. Very few do, and when they do, it's usually a sign that it's over. When we develop parasocial relationships, one-sided bonds where a person feels emotionally connected to a media figure like a celebrity or influencer, we internalize what they present and begin living in an alternate reality. We're constantly in search of perfection. So let me repeat it: perfect relationships do not exist.

And more so, when we're exposed to the drama in a never-ending collection of TV episodes, we subconsciously take on the belief that our relationships should have drama too. Over time, we start to feel that our relationships, even those that are completely healthy, are boring in comparison. The result? We subconsciously create drama and toxic patterns in our own relationships.

When we encounter normal, inevitable issues within our own relationships, we become disillusioned and discouraged, and we're less likely to work through them because we've consumed so much noise from social media. Over time, that noise becomes social cues that, when consumed over and over, quickly become implicit attitudes and behaviors. We can't build a strong, lasting relationship. We don't know how, and we start to wonder why. We blame the other person instead of taking a long, hard look at ourselves. When we do not understand why we do what we do in relationships, we destroy any relationship before it even starts.

Looking back on my past in conjunction with my research, two things become glaring. First, I was taught how to have relationships, but not explicitly or in a healthy way. I didn't learn how to engage with others successfully because of my upbringing, but according to my research, neither did most of us. Second, the ways by which we're socialized to engage in relationships are societal and familial, and both processes occur simultaneously and in an uncontrolled environment. Because we're exposed to so many dysfunctional relationships, we do not learn how to engage in them in a healthy manner, leaving many of us with no tools or skills to navigate potential problems. However, this doesn't mean you can use your past as a crutch. Take a deep look at your behaviors and how they might be affecting your relationships.

As you move through the next four chapters, pay attention to which of these channels shaped you most. The implicit beliefs that run underneath your awareness. The household you grew up watching. The direct experiences that left marks you are still carrying. That is where your pattern took root. By the time you reach Section II, you will be able to name it precisely. And naming it is where the real work begins.

What We Inherited

It's safe to say Americans date a little differently in 2026 than they did in the 50s and 60s. More and more couples meet on the internet, the marriage rate has fallen significantly over the last 40 years, and couples are waiting longer and longer before tying the knot.

I'm not promoting this as a good or a bad thing. It's simply the reality we have to acknowledge. Your relationship might look different than that of your parents or older role models. Our ideas, beliefs, and expectations about what a relationship should look like are definitely in need of a remodel in order to fit the modern cultural framework society is shifting toward.

So what is that shift, and how much have things changed? To accurately answer that, we must first investigate what a traditional relationship is. And most importantly, how can we shift our ideas about traditional relationships to fit into our modern cultural framework?

Traditional Relationships

Think about your parents, couples in older TV shows, or older couples you know. How do they interact with one another? What do you notice? What's different or alike? Do they have set responsibilities? Are mothers and fathers expected to perform certain roles? How would your father feel if your mother made more money than him?

Traditional relationships, like those you often see in older couples, are characterized by the idea that both parties will be completely monogamous and committed to each other for life. Within that context, there is a strong emphasis on exclusivity and faithfulness. Exclusivity is thought to equate to trust, but really, it equates to protection from other forces that threaten a relationship's stability. This is the very reason why our government and religious entities call marriage the Institution of Marriage. An institution is a complex organization that serves the needs, wants, and desires of a group of people with a set number of customs, beliefs, and traditions in an effort to uphold its place in society. Marriage is often seen as a way to formalize and strengthen the bond that creates a structured, stable, and secure environment. Understanding these two definitions is important because it gives us a strong foundation for why traditional relationships have maintained a power dynamic in yesterday's society while shifting toward a new dynamic in today's.

Additionally, traditional relationships focus on commitment. Both partners are expected to be 100% dedicated to the other and to work together if problems arise. Traditional couples are expected to make sacrifices and compromises, like taking on jobs they might not enjoy, spending more time on additional household responsibilities, or up and moving to a new, unfamiliar city. Stability and security are powerful tools in this institution for building a relationship, as are support and connection. We all want to feel loved and protected, right? However, the traditional relationship model lends itself to serious challenges given certain shifts in our culture today.

A common issue in traditional relationships is boredom or complacency. As couples grow familiar with each other and establish a routine, they grow bored. They wake up at the same time, head to work, make dinner, and things seem like a given. They lose the spark that initially attracted them to one another, and over time, the spark darkens completely, leading to dissatisfaction, which threatens a relationship's stability.

Power dynamics are another problem in traditional relationships. Traditionally, one partner takes on a more dominant role while the other takes on a more submissive, domestic role. This worked in the past, albeit poorly, but today the model falls apart. The traditional power dynamic leads to power imbalances, and over time, these imbalances turn into tension and hardships that modern couples can't get past.

The Stain of Patriarchy and Gender Roles

The stubborn persistence of patriarchy has caused great concern within the modern relationship dynamic and directly opposes gender equality. Patriarchy is man's demand to present their exclusive vision regardless of, and at the detriment of, women. My position is this: traditional relationships are outdated and rooted in patriarchy, and over time, women have upheld this vision by teaching the same system to their children, both boys and girls.

Although we've taken great strides toward gender equality, it is important to remember that women gained the right to vote just a little over 100 years ago. Feminist movements still work to force men, who solely benefit from patriarchal relationship models, to take their hands off women's autonomy. It is deeply researched and widely documented that men benefit from a traditional relationship model far more than their counterparts. Of course, this varies by region and country, but by and large, it is certainly universal.

Here's the thing though: even men are walking away from the institution, because as society shifts, it no longer benefits them either. Men are opting out of marriage at increasing rates. They're refusing to subscribe to a system that told them their value was contingent on what they could provide. When the people the institution was designed to serve start leaving, that tells you everything you need to know about whether it's working or not.

Gender roles lend themselves to certain performative positions that each party occupies. Traditional relationships operate on strict role expectations, varying depending on where you live and your cultural background. If these expectations aren't followed, panic and chaos ensue. Why? Because the stability of traditional relationships relies heavily on strict roles in order to maintain the existing power structure.

While these roles and expectations can provide a sense of structure and stability in a relationship, they can also create difficulties if one partner feels they are being asked to fulfill a role that does not fit with their personality, preferences, or desires.

The Pitfalls of a Traditional Relationship

My father grew up in the Baptist Church domination, and the church's ideals, especially regarding the scriptures' dictations of the sanctity of marriage, heavily affected his view of relationships. He grew up in a struggling single-parent home with ten siblings but was later adopted by a deeply religious married couple. Between his religious beliefs and background, as well as his exposure to a healthy marriage while he was still young, he adopted a traditional ideology when it came to marriage and performative gender roles.

My father believes in men's traditional gender roles, especially regarding protection, financial responsibility, leadership, and decision-making. However, he was always a little more lenient regarding women's traditional roles, including cleaning, cooking, and household chores. He believes in consulting his partner in terms of household decisions but ensures he has the final say. His beliefs have evolved over the years, but I hesitate to call them flexible or modern.

Although he is traditional and religious, when it comes to relationships, he's been married three times, with the first two marriages resulting in divorce. I don't think he internalized the "til death do us part" line in his traditional vows. I say this because divorce is where my father detaches from the traditional and religious model. He believes that when a relationship isn't working, one must roll up their sleeves and put in work to fix things, even if that means couples therapy, no matter how hard it may be. However, he maintains the position that if that's not enough, it's time to consider divorce. With two divorces under his belt, he has proven he will make that difficult decision when he has to.

Regardless of how modern his views are on divorce, he tried his best to raise me with his traditional beliefs, going as far as to push his religious beliefs about marriage onto me more times than I can count. He often quoted scripture when discussing dating, couples, and marriage. Although I believed what he'd taught me at the time, I knew his ideas weren't those I planned to adopt in my own relationships. And let me tell you, he often stressed his disappointment with me about this.

I remember him saying, "Carlos, life is like a buffet. You take what you like, and you leave on the table what's not for you." As it turns out, most of the things I left on the table were traditional, and to him, that was a huge problem. Not because he lacked understanding. He has two doctorate degrees. Rather, our implicit attitudes on an unconscious level more often than not control what we think and how we see the world. He would point his finger at issues in my relationships, saying I disregarded what he taught me and didn't follow his lead. What he really meant was his traditional lead. He readily agrees he's a traditional guy but also believes his ideas work for him and millions of others. To him, there's no need to fix what's not broken.

But is it really not broken? Or does he, like many men, benefit from patriarchy, thereby making it impossible to see its brokenness?

Don't get me wrong. My father taught me how to be a man, a good man, a man who understands how to treat a woman, care for her, protect her, and provide for her physically, emotionally, and financially. He uniquely understands the power of navigating through hard times without isolating his partner. He's a selfless, loving man who showed me by word and example that masculinity should not be toxic.

My father isn't perfect by any means, but he does have a strong understanding of traditional relationships and their role in past and present society. I can't definitively say that his emphasis on traditional relationships led to his divorces, but I can't say they didn't. What I can say is this: the traditional ideologies he instilled in me didn't work in my relationships, and I think it's reasonable to say this would be true for many modern couples.

Furthermore, despite our society's growing pressure to change traditional gender roles, many of us still maintain a genetic and evolutionary attraction to stereotypically feminine or masculine partners, signifying a steadfast adherence to traditional gender roles.

Many women and men in heterosexual relationships remain attracted to traditionally masculine or feminine characteristics, and I fully understand that from a cultural perspective here in America. But in many cultures around the world, these types of characteristics are entirely nonexistent.

The Aka people of Central Africa, the Mosuo people of China, and the Bugis people of Indonesia are just a few of many examples. I've heard my friends reiterate the phrase "tall, dark, and handsome" more times than I care to count, or the one I hate the most: "I want a manly man." Well okay, Sarah, what the hell is that supposed to mean?

However, research shows that the relationships of men and women with traditional gender roles are far from optimal. Over time, in our modern society, strictly adhering to traditional gender roles leads to serious problems in a relationship. Studies show that those who adhere to this model often experience more discontent and are less happy than their counterparts.

Here is what the traditional relationship model actually builds in the people raised inside it.

The Rescuer comes from households where love was earned through performance and service. Where the good child was the helpful child. Where worth was something you demonstrated, not something you simply had. The traditional model is one of the primary factories for that pattern because it teaches, from the very beginning, that love is conditional on what you provide.

The Escapist often comes from households where emotional expression inside rigid role structures was punished or dismissed. Where the rules were clear and the feelings were not supposed to show. Where going small and going quiet was how you stayed safe. The model did not create the wound. But it gave it a structure to live inside.

This is not an indictment of your parents or the culture they were raised in. They gave you what they had. It is simply the recognition that the blueprint you are carrying did not appear by accident. It was handed to you. And understanding that is the beginning of being able to set it down.

The Development of Modern Relationships

So how have things changed specifically? Modern couples are more likely to live together prior to getting married, and one of the consequences has been that marriage rates have steadily declined. Additionally, fewer people are getting remarried after divorce, and the divorce rate has steadily decreased in the last ten years. Not because marriages are working so well, but rather because fewer people are getting married before the age of 30. We no longer see a need to get married young, likely due to women's increased participation in the workforce and increased educational and financial independence. Increasingly more women pursue careers, so traditional household roles are no longer relevant. Women are taking control of their lives in ways that our grandparents could have only imagined. Partnerships are now equal. Both parties share responsibilities and have power over decisions. And research shows that it's working.

Online dating is another factor. Studies show that about 39% of adult couples met through online dating in 2017,[1] and the number has skyrocketed since then. It's likely online dating will eventually become the norm. Some people think online dating is a bad thing. Critics say it removes the emotional connection from the dating experience, but it does not. Online dating allows users to meet potential partners from a wide variety of backgrounds, leading to diverse relationships and dynamics. I would go further to add that online dating removes the bullshit and saves time. It forces potential partners to ask essential questions to determine compatibility. When I say "the one," I'm referring to the one right now. I do not believe in soulmates. Online dating promotes real, genuine conversations instead of googly-eyed, sexually motivated interactions and a real opportunity to see the other person for who they are at the beginning.

The term "soulmate" may be appealing and romantic, but it is a cultural and societal construct with no scientific backing. People are complex and multifaceted. It's unrealistic to believe that there is only one person capable of meeting our needs and desires. Furthermore, this idea creates unnecessary pressure and unrealistic expectations in relationships. There are over 8 billion people on earth. I am not convinced, and neither should you be, that only 1 out of 8 billion people was created specifically for us. The math just doesn't add up.

Today, there are no preset roles in relationships other than those explicitly defined by the individuals in the partnership. In other words, both partners are expected to provide equal value. My partner and I must work, pay bills, make decisions equally, and split chores around the house, with the exception of washing the dishes, a chore I despise with a burning passion. That's likely connected to childhood trauma that I refuse to address because I've decided it's more useful as an excuse to avoid doing the dishes. But that's a story for another time.

SIDEBAR: Did you know that there are some traumas we experience that we can process and work through but choose not to? It's because of the behavioral habits these experiences created. They serve negative patterns and dysfunctions and provide us the excuses we need to continue in our own bullshit.

Modern relationships and their dynamics are a strong and necessary departure from those we traditionally engaged in. Traditional relationships follow clear-cut gender roles, whereas modern relationships are more fluid and flexible. Modern relationships also take homosexual and non-monogamous relationship models into account. They are characterized by open communication and understanding, and they prioritize emotional connection over support or reliance.

Because modern relationships require open communication, both members are expected to listen to their partner and adequately communicate their own needs. Social, cultural, and technological advances change the way we experience relationships, and we're more satisfied as a result.

Now more than ever, relationships are characterized by equality, flexibility, and individuality. Partners support the well-being of the other as well as their own. Because parties occupy multiple roles at once and gender roles aren't as much of a factor, tasks, duties, and responsibilities are more equal, and those participating in modern relationships are more satisfied with the dynamic than their traditional relationship counterparts. No one feels left out of decisions, no one feels overworked and overwhelmed, and each person has their needs met. Both partners are expected to contribute to the relationship in terms of emotional and practical support, decision-making, and responsibilities. Traditional gender roles aren't adhered to in modern relationships and aren't clearly defined. Both parties do the work.

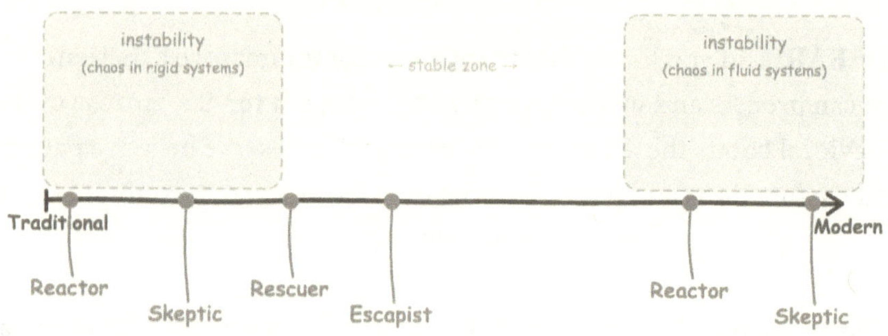

Modern Monogamy

Monogamy is the practice of having only one sexual or romantic partner at a time. Pretty simple, right? However, monogamy and its definition have changed significantly over the years, and our modern practice of monogamy is much different than the way our parents, grandparents, and ancestors practiced it.

Historically, monogamy was a social and religious idea. Many cultures and world religions promoted the idea that individuals should have one sexual and romantic partner in a lifetime. In many cases, this idea was motivated by beliefs in the sanctity of marriage and the importance of fidelity. In other cases, traditional monogamy was driven by concerns of property and monetary inheritance. People had to make sure that their wealth and assets were passed to legitimate heirs.

Despite the prevalence of monogamy in social and religious ideals, it wasn't always practiced. In many cultures, polygamy, the practice of having multiple sexual and romantic partners, was very common, especially within wealthy and powerful circles. Sometimes our predecessors engaged in multiple relationships at once. In other cases, they might have had a series of monogamous relationships one after another.

Today, the meaning and practice of monogamy are a bit different. Before, monogamy meant being with one person for a lifetime. Now, it means being with one person at a time. Many societies have nearly abandoned monogamy as a religious or social requirement. People are free to choose whether or not they want to have one sexual or romantic partner at a time. As a result, monogamy has become more of a personal choice rather than a social or religious one. This shift toward chosen monogamy reflects other cultural shifts. Our ideas about sexuality are different, and so are our ideas about diverse relationship structures.

One of the main reasons for that shift is the awareness and demand for women's sexual freedom. As women continue to chip away at the patriarchal stronghold over their autonomy, society begins to see that patriarchy told women that sex was only to be used for the benefit of a man, at little to no pleasure for her.

For hundreds, if not thousands, of years, millions of women had no idea they were capable of having an orgasm. Many women were taught that it was taboo to touch themselves and explore their own bodies. In fact, women in certain communities, especially those of a patriarchal hierarchy or religious background, were taught that masturbation was synonymous with the words slutty and ungodly.

Think about the word pleasure. We often associate it with sex, and I hear people use the term "guilty pleasure" far more than I hear the word "pleasure" on its own, and I think this is quite telling. Men used women's bodies as a warm, cozy dumping ground for their own pleasure, and women were expected to sit down and take it, both literally and figuratively. Men cared about their own pleasure for selfish reasons, not the pleasure of their partner. Society and its patriarchal foundations defined expectations that women shouldn't be in charge of their own sexuality. Their bodies were bedroom tools for men.

As women begin to release the stigma of their sexuality, the more they gain an awareness of their bodies, and it's this awareness that releases them from antiquated ideas about their sexual expression. As they adopt a more modern, liberated idea of sex, women view monogamy differently. They're free to choose whether or not to engage in monogamy or to abandon the notion altogether.

Modern monogamy is a perfectly valid way to engage in a relationship and often provides couples stability and trust. There are many ways to practice modern monogamy, so let's get into that now.

Monogamy might look like an unmarried couple who have each agreed to be completely exclusive romantically and sexually. They've communicated and come to the mutual understanding that monogamy is the best choice for them, and they're committed to maintaining this standard in their relationship.

Monogamy might also look like an individual who's not in a romantic relationship, but who has made a choice to remain sexually exclusive with their partner. They have their reasons, but they've decided this is the best choice for their mental and physical well-being.

Lastly, a person who's in a situationship, friends with benefits, or a sexual or romantic relationship that isn't defined, who decides to remain monogamous with the other person, is also a practice thereof.

Monogamy exists in multiple forms, and each is completely valid. It's your choice, and your choice is valid regardless of what society may think or feel.

Non-Monogamous Relationships

Gender equality and the acknowledgment of LGBTQIA+ rights both contribute to our acceptance of non-traditional relationships. We don't talk about non-monogamous couples in hushed tones anymore. Instead, we discuss them openly, for the most part. As society continues to be open-minded regarding the discussion of non-traditional relationships, we also begin to discuss relationship structures that aren't monogamous. These structures work too, because one size does not fit all.

Consensual non-monogamy refers to relationships where all romantic partners make a decision to engage in other sexual or romantic relationships while remaining in a relationship with the other consenting partner.

Consensual non-monogamy takes a few different forms. Some couples might decide that one or both people engage in romantic relationships with others, but not sexual relationships. In other cases, they might decide to engage in sexual relationships with others but not romantic ones. Some couples engage in consensual non-monogamous relationships to fill sexual, romantic, and personal needs. Their reasons for doing so are entirely their own. There are different ways to form and structure a relationship, and no one has the right to judge another person's decision.

The couple's agreement varies from couple to couple and from person to person, but each model, however adopted, is built on communication and trust. Both people adhere to specific rules they agree on, which is why they're consensual. Non-consensual non-monogamy is widely referred to as cheating, so agreement and understanding are important.

In other words, modern monogamy is a choice, not a requirement.

Exercise: The Inherited Blueprint Map:
https://go.carloshines.com/book/blueprint-map
or Scan the QR Code below

Situationships

Drew was lying on his bed, phone in hand. "Hey," Mia said, setting her purse, stuffed with an extra pair of panties and jeans, on the carpet and walking over to the bed.

"Hey," he asked, "how was work?"

"Alright," she propped herself up on one of his pillows. "Annie is on my ass this week."

"Are things almost ready for release?" He looked her over for a moment. He liked the way she looked after work. Most people might have thought of her as strait-laced, but there was something about her that Drew found intriguing.

"Almost, just some coding issues at the moment." She paused, looking him over as he'd done to her. "How about you?"

"Same shit different day," he replied. Mia played with the ends of her dark hair and stared at him flirtatiously. Neither of them said anything for a moment, but the sexual tension grew stronger. Mia looked down at her legs, splayed out on the bed. They sat in silence, looking at each other for a few seconds.

"I need a shower," Drew said, raising his eyebrows. He was chaotic in a way Mia found undeniably sexy.

"What kinda shower?" She let a smile run across her lips and outlined them with her finger.

"Our kind of shower," he muttered.

Misty fog permeated the bathroom, but at that moment, which wasn't a moment but the better part of an hour, Drew didn't care about the water bill. He let his hands roam Mia's body, embracing each divot. Mia, in turn, played with him for a bit, kissing him briefly before pulling away. Drew grew frustrated by this, but Mia liked to make him a little angry because she knew it made him more sexually aggressive and she loved everything about rough sex. Mia let out loud moans, but each was punctuated by a spanking sound as she bent over, bracing herself against the faucet. The two giggled after each spank in a comfortable way. Drew made sure Mia had several orgasms before his big release. They'd been sleeping together like this for nearly six months, but they'd been good friends for years.

The two emerged after an hour, Mia with small, budding hickeys on her chest like a love struck teenager, and Drew with a massive, almost childlike smile on his face. She wrapped herself in a towel and began drying her hair with another in front of the fog, and Drew wrapped his arms around her waist, pressing himself against her back and kissing her neck.

They laid in bed later that night, cocooned in Drew's sheets. Mia glanced over at his phone and noticed his Tinder app was absent from his homepage, where it had always sat. "You deleted Tinder?" she asked, confused. She recoiled for a moment.

"Yeah," he replied, "why?"

"Well why did you delete it?" she asked, putting her phone down next to her.

"I found my match," he said jovially, delighted by his own statement. What the fuck? Mia asked herself. She thought of the date she'd gone on with the self-proclaimed entrepreneur she met last week. Then she thought of the other date she went on last night. She sat up in bed, Drew's eyes still following her. This wasn't part of the deal, she thought to herself.

"What?" she asked with a taut tone. The sex is great, Mia thought before muttering, "Okay," sarcastically.

"Did you delete Tinder?" Drew said, sounding a little tremulous. "Or Bumble or whatever." He'd said something he shouldn't have. He was certain of it.

"I didn't," said Mia. She looked at Drew's face. His expression had moved from excited to anxious to nervous to reserved in a matter of moments, finally landing on a combination of apprehensive confusion and dismay. His eyes appeared tired, much more fatigued than they had when she'd arrived. He was consciously trying not to show her any more emotional vulnerability than his body language had already revealed.

"So, you're still dating?"

"Yeah," Mia paused, "I am." Drew looked away from her and opened the drawer on his bedside table. His hands shook like a leaf in October. "You don't want me to lie, right?" Mia said, trying to salvage Drew's ego. She'd noticed a vulnerability in him that she hadn't seen before. "We didn't talk about it. I'm not ready to do that yet. I wish you would've told me you wanted that. I didn't lie." She looked at his face, waiting for a reply that didn't come. "We're in different places right now. We want different things."

"We didn't talk about it. That's true." He looked reserved, but not in a good way. "But why didn't you tell me any of this?" he asked, searching her face for an answer she couldn't provide. She looked back at him, silent. He picked up his phone from the nightstand and said, "I think it would be best if you left."

Mia pulled on her joggers and left, but not before muttering a small "sorry" before locking the door behind her.

What you just read was not a story about miscommunication. It was a story about two nervous systems operating from completely different survival strategies. One person moved toward connection. The other maintained distance. Neither of them chose those strategies consciously. They built them.

By Section II, you will have the language for exactly what happened in that bathroom and that bed. For now, notice which one you recognized yourself in. That recognition is the beginning of something.

Mia and Drew were in what's called a situationship: a romantic or sexual relationship that is not defined or committed, nor is there any explicit agreement between the participants. They might also be described as noncommittal dating relationships which teeter between committed relationships and casual dating. They are often sexual in nature, undefined, and may involve conflicting expectations and misunderstandings. They are often referred to as friends with benefits, and I use these terms interchangeably. Some research indicates that situationships and open relationships teeter along the same line.

Open relationships are, by definition, committed relationships in which both partners agree to have other sexual or romantic partners outside of the primary relationship. Open relationships come with a certain stigma. Contrary to popular belief, open relationships, or consensual non-monogamous relationships, are not cheating. One study examining the dynamics and viability of open relationships showed that 73% of those in open relationships reported that their decision to enter into the relationship was mutual. The same study noted that open relationships' emphasis relies on rules and mutual commitment.

There are some open relationships that are well-situated. They include strict rules, responsibilities, and open communication. Both partners mutually benefit. In my coaching practice, the number of open relationships that fit these guidelines is 2 out of 10, and they work great.

However, the other 8 couples think they are in open relationships but, in reality, they are not. These other eight couples set rules that benefit one partner and not the other. They also create rules that are surface-level, vague, and leave too much room for miscommunication or huge loopholes that are detrimental to the relationship. It is because of these circumstances, which are the norm and not the exception, that I call open relationships nothing but glorified situationships.

Situationships and open relationships have many commonalities. Both types of relationships involve a certain degree of openness and non-exclusivity, and both can be either casual or serious.

One of the main challenges is that they can be difficult to navigate, and communication is often lackluster, if not nonexistent. Because the relationship is not clearly defined, it can be difficult for both partners to communicate their expectations and boundaries, leading directly to conflict. Mia and Drew hadn't defined their relationship status. Mia had continued dating other people, and Drew was under the impression the two were monogamous. Because they hadn't clearly defined the nature of their relationship, the two arrived at the intersection of misunderstanding and conflict, one they were unable to effectively navigate.

Furthermore, the individuals in them often do not feel the need to openly communicate with each other due to their lack of commitment. They don't feel like they owe the other person an explanation for their actions. This can be especially difficult for those accustomed to a traditional, monogamous relationship model or for those who are not familiar with the inner workings of a situationship, which is most of us. In the example, Mia did feel a need to explain herself but still did not feel a need to define the relationship or work through the misunderstanding. Drew was under the impression they were practicing monogamy, while Mia believed they were operating under a more open, non-monogamous model. A situationship, or for that matter, any relationship without open, honest communication becomes messy. We can't build a house on sand and expect it to have a firm foundation.

The Transactionality of Relationships

Here's where it gets uncomfortable, because what I'm about to say applies to all of us, not just Mia, and not just the people in situationships. It applies to the way most of us enter any relationship, defined or not.

We go into relationships to take, not to give. At least in the beginning.

I know that's not a comfortable thing to read, but sit with it. No one goes into a new relationship saying, "I am going to give them my everything. I'll cook and clean and take them on fun romantic dates." At least, no one I know. So don't try to manipulate yourself into believing you're the exception to the take-not-give rule.

We enter a relationship to see what the other person can offer us. We ask, "What do we get out of being with this person?" and "What are they bringing to the table?" My mother's own ideas about relationships were built on transactionality. She made it clear to her partners that they were to give, and she was to receive. I loved my mother, and I saw her point of view, but she was wrong. I know many other people who share this view, though few remain forthright about it. We see another person based on what they can do for us, and this is a phenomenon many of us hold, particularly in the earlier stages of a relationship. Let me caution you though: this attitude will always lead to a lopsided relationship that ends in trauma.

Here's another example. I have a friend who loves Tinder, but she refuses to match with anyone who doesn't have the words doctor, lawyer, or banker in their profile. She expects expensive dates to exclusive Manhattan restaurants, and if her partner asks her to go Dutch, she leaves them on read. The irony is that she isn't in any of those professions. She certainly isn't alone, though this is an extreme example. She prefers to get more than she gives, and she and many others like it this way. It has nothing to do with the old cliche of being a gold digger. In this instance, it is purely transactional. How long do you think she can sustain a relationship using this dynamic?

Our give and take ideology doesn't stop at romantic relationships. Many people view platonic relationships similarly, whether they admit it or not. We go into relationships to take, not give. At least in the beginning.

But does this transactional dynamic change over the course of a relationship? Most definitely, depending on the person. Over time we form concrete, tangible attachments toward another person, and trust becomes a larger factor. In short, we give what we get because our feelings about the other person become deeper and more emotional. We become more selfless. Love, then, is not self-seeking, and it does not keep a record.

Nevertheless, our give and take beliefs are part of the reason why situationships work so well. We're provided the opportunity to appeal to our inherently selfish, all-about-me traits. This is neither a good nor bad thing. I believe situationships to be a valid relationship model if it works for you. What matters is being conscious of the psychological mechanisms that rest behind the curtain of our behaviors within sexual and romantic relationships.

Let's take a step back. There are other key components and similarities beyond universal transactionality which govern both situationships and open relationships, and these include emotional connection and intimacy. Both arrangements involve some level of emotional connection between the two partners, and intimacy is nearly always part of the equation. Either model can be defined as casual or serious, depending on the expectations of both individuals involved. Mia and Drew cared about one another and asked about each other's work, clearly demonstrating a level of familiarity with one another's lives and schedules. Intimacy was a large part of their relationship, perhaps the largest part, but they interacted on a regular basis and held an emotional connection, albeit a convoluted one, toward one another.

We have yet to discuss emotional difficulty, a key drawback of the situationship model. Drew was clearly upset when he learned that Mia was still dating other people. While we don't know how long Drew had been under the impression that they were monogamous, we can assume he was taking his beliefs seriously. Deleting Tinder was a big step. Their dating environment hinged on immediacy and availability. So when they made themselves unavailable by deleting Tinder, or in Mia's case, choosing not to, they were each making a statement about where they stood. When situationships are not clearly defined, partners may feel uncertain about their status with one another and the future of the relationship. This can lead to feelings of insecurity and anxiety, causing some partners to become emotionally attached despite the lack of commitment. There's nothing wrong with emotional attachment. We're human, and we crave connection. But when that attachment isn't properly communicated, one party might leave feeling used or neglected.

Despite these challenges, situationships can be a positive and fulfilling experience for some people. Studies show that those seeking them were interested in getting to know others romantically as opposed to just sex, directly opposing many people's preconceptions about them. However, the same studies show a difference in gender in response to the question, "Why did you enter into a situationship?" Male participants were more likely to want to experience new things and were interested in sexual satisfaction, while the women studied wanted to feel free. Many individuals who are not ready for a committed relationship, like Mia, or those who are not interested in monogamy, seek out a situationship as a way to explore their sexuality and romantic desires without the pressures that come with commitment.

Dynamics and Emotions Within Situationships

The dynamics of a situationship vary greatly depending on the individuals involved and their expectations for the relationship. Their emotions can be complex and quite varied. Partners may experience a wide range of feelings, from uncertainty and confusion to attachment and jealousy. Some common dynamics and emotions that may be involved in a include:

Uncertainty and ambiguity: Because their boundaries are not clearly defined, both partners may feel uncertain about the status and future of the relationship. They are usually operated on a day-by-day basis. Most conversations are surface level at best because they lack the boldness to have serious conversations. This often leads to confusion and insecurity and may cause partners to question whether or not they're on the same page.

Conflicting expectations: Since they are not explicitly negotiated, partners usually have different expectations for the relationship. This will lead to misunderstandings and conflicts, especially if one partner wants a more serious or committed relationship while the other is looking for something non-monogamous and open.

As I delved deeper into this topic, it became apparent that the real issue here is that we do not explicitly ask what our partners' expectations are. Instead, we assume that our expectations align just because we consented to the romantic or sexual nature of the relationship. This is, in fact, a ticking time bomb.

Emotional attachment: Despite the lack of commitment, partners in them still develop strong emotional feelings for each other. Intimacy breeds emotional connection. There's no way to circumvent that reality. Unfortunately, this can be especially challenging if one partner wants to move the relationship forward while the other does not. This is where I often see situationships turn highly emotional and downright ugly. Often, we like to say things like "it's just sex," "there are no feelings here," and "we're just having fun." It's all fun and games until someone catches feelings.

Jealousy and insecurity: Considering that situationships are not exclusive, partners may worry about the other person's interactions with other people. Think back to our example. While we cannot say definitively what happened after Mia left, we can assume Drew wasn't happy after he found out about her seeing other people, which was the main reason he asked her to leave. He felt insecure and uneasy. Worrying about the other partner's additional relationships can lead to feelings of jealousy and insecurity, which may require open communication and negotiation to resolve. However, in these scenarios, usually the only resolution is to end it. There is no foreseeable success in a situationship with turned-up emotions that breed jealousy and insecurity.

Emotions are not the only complicating factor within situationships. We haven't touched on race or gender in this context, but we cannot enter into a discussion regarding the situationship or friends-with-benefits model without a thorough conversation about the role that racial and ethnic background plays in the development and sustainability of a situationship. Many studies looking at the validity of situationships and other open relationship models focus on white individuals, particularly white women, causing a false narrative within the research available.

I found one decidedly inclusive study of Black women in situationships. The study found that situationships operate within a gray space, a place of in-betweenness, in which Black women attempt to gain the girlfriend identity by starting out in a sexual situationship. The research concluded that situationships generally provide a false sense of progression into committed relationships for Black women, and that through exhibiting behaviors of emphasized femininity and hegemonic masculinity, situationships appear to be oppressive to Black women's sexual agency but are beneficial to men. Additionally, Black women sometimes find themselves being tested by the other person, especially within heterosexual relationships, to find out if they're what some might call girlfriend material.

Let's make this plain. The study proves that Black women who allow themselves to participate in friends-with-benefits, situationship, or open relationship dynamics more often than not are manipulating themselves into believing that there could be something more, that it can grow into a full-blown committed relationship. But that just isn't the reality, because research has proven that males are the sole benefactors of situationships in most cases.

While these women are using a temporary situation in hopes that it will become a long-term committed relationship, the men they're with are using these temporary situations in hopes that they will stay as temporary as possible. They avoid commitment while specifically focusing on keeping their sexual needs satisfied. To do this, some men will take you on emotional roller coasters, lie to your face, and swear that they're just not ready for commitment, when in reality, they are holding on to you long enough to find your replacement.

I'll be straight with you here, because I promised at the beginning of this book that I would be. As I've taught my only daughter: I'll never sugarcoat the truth. I'll give you the information. What you do with it is up to you. Men, if any of what I just said makes you feel some kind of way, good. Use that feeling as an opportunity to reevaluate yourself and your priorities. Better yet, use it as an opportunity to do better.

If you're thinking of the word patriarchy, you're right. Historically, Black women and other women of color suffer from patriarchal labels that characterize them as hypersexual vixens or promiscuous. Society uses these untrue, harmful stereotypes to assert that women, particularly women of color, are inferior to men, and to eliminate their sexual and bodily autonomy. Patriarchy only benefits men and allows them sexual control over women's bodies. We can conclude, based on this study and the few others available, that because of these stereotypes, Black women generally do not benefit from the situationship model.

I am by no means saying that Black women shouldn't enter into a situationship, but to do so, we must be conscious of the misguided prejudices and archaic stereotypes perpetuated by our historically racist, patriarchal society. As long as you are aware of the above factors, you can absolutely make a situationship or friends with benefits work in your favor rather than against you.

Situationships Turned Relationships

To begin a discussion about how situationships might become conventional relationships, we must examine how relationships form in the first place. Little research is available regarding the pathway to relationships, and our ideas about relationship formation are heterosexist in nature. Consider the meet-cute, an idea perpetuated by modern romantic comedies. In a meet-cute, two people meet haphazardly at a coffee shop, or library, or waiting in line at a busy take-out establishment. One individual drops a book, keys, or a bag, and the other reaches to grab it. Their hands touch, and boom: it's love at first sight. If you're thinking that's so cute, think again. In most cases, romance is derived from a long-term friendship, not a meet-cute.

Cultural scripts or structures that organize how we understand and interpret life events influence our ideas of what is normal and extend to our perceptions of relationship formation. Our heteronormative and heterosexist Western cultural script dictates a long list of stereotyped actions we should take when entering into a romantic relationship. Men are expected to use bold and direct behaviors to make their interest known to women, while women focus on making themselves attractive and waiting for men to make a move. Our cultural dating script is highly sexist, trapping women and men in performative social positions they do not truly occupy. Relationship science is ultimately hindered by our implicit heterosexist society. Despite convincing evidence that passion-based intimacy can arise from friendship-based intimacy among same-gender friends, it may not have occurred to researchers that such a thing could also happen in platonic friendships between heterosexual men and women. However, other studies show that people often know one another for months or even years before they officially enter couplehood, and this research extends to people of all genders.

Furthermore, our heteronormative society overlooks relationships that begin as simple friendships for the sole reason that many believe men and women cannot possibly be friends without becoming sexually attracted to one another, when this is far from the case. The way we view relationship formation reflects an ideology that values and prioritizes heterosexual relationships while stigmatizing and marginalizing non-heterosexual ways of being, despite cultural shifts toward the de-stigmatization of LGBTQIA+ relationships and nontraditional ones. This research ultimately disproves the meet-cute model and illustrates a gap between our heterosexist society's biases and our reality.

It is ultimately possible and normal for couples to start as friends before initiating a romantic relationship. Both situationships and committed relationships primarily form this way. Think back to Mia and Drew. They were friends for years before entering into a friends-with-benefits relationship model. Think about your own friends and family members' intimate relationships. I'm sure you can find several that began as friendships.

It is possible for situationships to turn into committed relationships, although I highly recommend against it. Because situationships are not explicitly defined or negotiated, partners may have different expectations and desires for the relationship should it become more serious. As a result, this can make it difficult for the relationship to progress and may even cause long-term conflicts or misunderstandings.

If both partners are committed to turning the situationship into a serious, dedicated relationship, they will need to maintain open and honest communication about their expectations and boundaries, which is something they might not be necessarily used to within the situationship. Clear, strong communication can establish a clearer definition of the relationship and can pave the way for a more serious and successful committed partnership.

However, it is also important for partners to be realistic about the potential for a situationship to turn into a committed relationship. The word potential is important. If one partner is not interested in committing at this time, or if the partners have conflicting expectations for the relationship, it may be best to end the situationship rather than try to force it into a committed relationship. Here are some parameters that signal when it is or isn't possible.

When It's Just Not Possible

Even when communication is clear, maintained, and defined, it is still not always possible for situationships to develop into committed relationships. I've seen this situation several times in my life and far too many times throughout my practice. Here are some of the primary reasons:

Different expectations: As mentioned previously, expectations within situationships are often not explicitly defined or negotiated, which can lead to conflicting expectations between partners. If one partner wants a more serious and committed relationship while the other is not interested in progressing further, it may be difficult for the relationship to move forward. I often see one partner who is willing to compromise everything in order to have the one they desire. Usually, the desired one isn't willing to give up anything because they've become accustomed to being single while enjoying the benefits of a sexual situationship. They're having their cake and eating it too.

Incompatibility: Even if both partners are interested in a committed relationship, they may not be compatible in other ways that are important for building a successful relationship. People enter situationships for a variety of reasons, and it is safe to say that many enter into them for intimacy, not long-term commitment. Those who enter a situationship might not see a need to align their values, goals, and interests with the other person's.

Lack of commitment: In order for a committed relationship to work, both partners must be willing to commit to each other and to the relationship. Think back to Mia and Drew. Mia wasn't ready to commit, while Drew was ready and willing to move to a more serious, monogamous relationship model.

Outside factors: External factors, such as distance, work or school schedules, or other obligations, can make it difficult for a situationship to evolve into a committed relationship. In a situationship, it might not be a big deal if the two people live a few hours away from each other. They can hang out and be intimate whenever they feel the need without feeling obligated. But a relationship is entirely different. Partners need quality time with one another to trust each other and build a strong foundation. If one or both partners are unable to devote enough time and energy to the relationship, it will not be able to thrive.

The most common reason a situationship fails to convert into a relationship is not timing. It is not external circumstances. It is that the two people involved are running incompatible nervous system responses to intimacy. One moves toward. The other moves away. Without names for those responses, both people spend years blaming the situation or the other person's unavailability. The pattern was never unavailability. It was protection. And protection, without examination, will outlast every situationship and every relationship that follows.

Why It Can Work Out

Despite the challenges outlined above, it is possible for situationships to turn into committed relationships and work out successfully. Here is Imani and Alexia's success story.

Alexia sat in the corner of a crowded Italian restaurant, glancing over at the empty place setting next to her. It's already 6:15, she thought. Imani was late and she wasn't replying. She looked up for a moment, catching her friend, who wasn't so much her friend as her friend with benefits, Imani, rushing into the restaurant.

"Hey," Alexia paused. "Are you okay?" Imani sat down and grabbed the wine list sitting in the middle of the table, ignoring Alexia's question.

"Where's the waitress?" Imani asked, cutting in. "I need wine." She paused. "Right now."

Alexia took Imani's hand under the table. "Are you okay?"

"I'm exhausted," Imani began. "It's been a long week."

"I know," said Alexia, looking at Imani's face. She looks perfect, Alexia thought to herself. She admired this. Even after sex, Imani looked amazing. Their relationship had developed over the course of about a year. She'd met Imani on Bumble BFF. They didn't end up being BFFs, not in the traditional sense.

"I don't wanna talk about it." The waitress came over and Imani ordered a glass of wine.

"Imani," Alexia began before pausing. "We can talk about that stuff."

Imani glanced down at her menu. "There's shit with my sister and my roommate's a pig and I'm just..." She dropped the menu back on the table. Her silverware rattled a bit.

"I'll be your roommate," Alexia chuckled. Imani didn't appear pleased by her ever-jovial attitude. "Problem solved."

"Can you be serious just this once?" Imani said, rolling her eyes.

"Look, I get it," Alexia responded. "I know it's a lot."

"And to be honest, I'm having a tough time with this stuff," Imani muttered.

"What do you mean?" Alexia asked. Imani remained silent. "Oh," Alexia replied, hoping the waiter would come by to soften the tension. "You mean us."

"I wasn't gonna say it like that." Imani closed her menu. "But yeah, this."

"We talked about this a few months ago," Alexia said, thinking back to their conversation. They'd talked about their relationship status in the car on the way home from her favorite movie theater. "We weren't ready for anything. And, for the record, I'm okay with that."

"I know, it's just..." Imani paused. They'd talked about it, but there was something she'd forgotten to say. She'd left out the "I don't wanna sleep with other people anymore" part. "Honestly, I don't want you to see other people. I want us to be serious."

"And I really like you." Alexia waited a few moments before replying.

"I like you and I don't want us to have sex with other people either. I want to be more serious. I just thought you were."

"You thought wrong," Imani said. Alexia paused, slightly frustrated, slightly relieved. Imani continued, "You're one of the kindest people I know. You think about me." She paused again. "We want the same things. We both like living near an ocean and..."

"So, we're dating because we both like the beach?" Alexia laughed a bit.

"No," Imani told her. "It's the principle. And we both want kids and I just..."

"Kids already?" Alexia giggled, partly because she was uncomfortable.

"You know what I mean," Imani rolled her eyes. "I like you. I want this."

"So, we're not seeing other people?"

"We are not seeing other people." The two picked up their glasses in unison, clinked them in cheers, and took a brief sip, smiling at one another.

And that's what they did. Imani's lease ended the following month, and Alexia, who'd been looking to get out of her non-air-conditioned apartment for a year, moved right in.

Situationships can turn into successful, long-term relationships. However, it requires open communication, compatibility, commitment, and timing. I am by no means saying there are rules, but in my experience, building a relationship based on a situationship is no easy feat, especially when one partner isn't communicative toward another.

Imani and Alexia are a prime example of a couple in need of an open and honest conversation. Alexia was under the impression they weren't exclusive, emotionally or sexually, while Imani believed they both understood they were exclusive, causing a large rift in their relationship. Yet when they were able to communicate, they came to an understanding regarding how they wanted their relationship to progress.

Imani and Alexia's communication styles are drastically different. Imani isn't always honest or straightforward, preferring to beat around the bush to avoid confrontation. She doesn't joke or make light of things. Alexia, on the other hand, is a bit more direct but jokes when she feels uncomfortable. This is a workable problem, but both individuals in a functioning relationship must be aware of how they can communicate using their own preferences and those of their partner. When partners discuss ways to work through issues, they can build a strong foundation for their partnership.

Both Imani and Alexia seem relatively compatible. While wanting kids and living near the water aren't all that's necessary to determine compatibility, you can assume that the two of them share compatible values. They are comfortable with one another, desire similar lives, and value compassion. When I began writing this book, I checked in on them. I am happy to report that they are living together beautifully, took the time to learn one another's communication styles, and have put in the hard work it takes to build a solid foundation for their relationship. I am extremely proud of them.

Turning a situationship into a committed relationship is possible, but I don't recommend it. While blurred lines and expectations, communication barriers, and certain interests can be resolved or clarified, it is difficult to do, and many couples are not ready, nor do they have the tools necessary to do the challenging work in order to lay a solid foundation.

Exercise: The Expectation Audit:
https://go.carloshines.com/book/expectation-audit
or Scan the QR Code below

Is Love Really Blind?

Regardless of where we live, what we look like, our age, our professions, our socioeconomic classes, our personal backgrounds, or which identities we occupy, we all want the same thing: to be loved for who we are on the inside.

Dating and marriage reality shows are becoming increasingly mainstream, and, as a Relationship Expert and Researcher, I have many concerns about using television shows to find and explore potential partners. Not only that, but they perpetuate false narratives and stereotypes about relationships.

For now, let's discuss one that I both love and hate. It's a guilty pleasure of mine and simultaneously one of the most misleading things on television. The premise of the popular Netflix show *Is Love Blind?* is considered an experiment. Thirty singles, 15 men and 15 women, enter soundproofed pods where they then date without seeing their potential companions, leaving them to use the other person's voice, conversation skills, and tone to gauge their level of romantic interest. The participants are stripped of all distractions, including cell phones, and they live on-set with the rest of the show's participants, separated by gender. The show's focus is on connecting with other people. Participants are not permitted to touch one another, see one another, or ask about physical characteristics. However, they're afforded the opportunity to get to know one another through deep, meaningful conversations, the kind they've never indulged in with family members, friends, or those they've previously dated, stated by the show's executive producer.

The producers believe they are proving that an emotional connection, sight unseen, makes love truly blind. Clearly, they haven't done any research or spoken to professionals in the sociology, psychology, or relationship fields. If they had, they would have a clearer understanding of this concept: there is no such thing as blind love as it is performed in the show's process. What is presented on *Is Love Blind?* isn't blind love. Rather, it is an emotional attachment that preserves the participant's red flags, bad habits, and past traumas, and in many cases, disregards the couple's emotional reality. Few relationships formed on the show actually work out in the long run. These couples get so caught up in the idea that love is blind that they forget to ask key basic questions about what they want for the future regarding family, career, location of residence, and so on.

When I speak of blind love, I approach it from two perspectives. First, blind love, according to the societal definition, refers to putting on blinders and ignoring the realities of the person we are dating, specifically ignoring the red flags. Second, I refer to blind love within the context of trauma bonds that bind two people together for all the wrong reasons.

The cultural and proverbial meaning of "love is blind" is our irrevocable tendency to ignore any potential deficiencies in a partner, leaving us to see only sunbeams and magical rainbows. Should I caution you? Love isn't some heavenly magic trick. It's science.

What our culture considers blind love is a far cry from what sociology, psychology, and scientific research know it to be. Culturally, we view blind love as falling in love with someone's personality rather than their physical attributes. Think of the Disney movie *Beauty and the Beast*, the premise of which comes with its own set of connotations and issues. While this tale encourages us to value inner beauty, it also hints that transformation, whether in attitude or appearance, is somehow necessary for a happily ever after. This gives love an almost magical, redemptive quality, suggesting it can fundamentally change someone or reveal a true self. We tend to view love as a divine, overwhelming force that catches us by surprise and sweeps us away. I'm sorry to be the bearer of bad news, but there is no evidence of this type of blind love.

I want to share with you how blind love works from a scientific perspective so you may gain a stronger understanding while at the same time breaking down an untrue cultural myth. Why do I want to use precious page space to break this myth? Because our culture shoves myths about love down our throats. As we consume media, we start to believe these myths and unconsciously expect them to be performed in our lives, but in reality, love and relationships do not work in those ways.

According to scientists and researchers, love is, in some ways, blind. However, it is not blind in the sense that we value another person's personality so much that we're willing to abandon traditional notions of physical attraction. This is a fairy tale, one that is simply not true. There is strong evidence that love overpowers those areas of the brain that control critical thought, so when we get close to someone, the brain does not analyze the person's character, leaving us effectively blind to our partner's red flags. In other words, we tend to perceive possible romantic partners in an enhanced, even overly optimistic way. We ignore red flags.

However, it's complicated. Love can be blind in the scientific sense, yet also wedded to reality, primarily because love is a product of evolutionary forces designed to enhance humans' reproductive fitness. On one hand, we should choose partners in a logical manner to find someone with whom we are most compatible. On the other hand, we are compelled to see our partners in the best light to maintain established bonds critical to raising offspring successfully.

If we focus solely on the fact that our insides are bubbling with overly emotional feelings, our relationships will fail. If we see our relationship only through rose-colored glasses, we find long-term happiness much more difficult to cultivate. At its core, love is an evolutionary adaptation necessary to grow and maintain the human population.

Yes, love is scientifically blind, but certainly not in a cultural way. It is this blinding effect that allows us to mate with potential partners and produce offspring. Logic, bonding, and trust are key factors when considering staying in love. That's the goal, right? The scientific definition of blind love is entirely different from our culture's myths and expectations. So if we as a culture are willing to use the term, let's begin to use it in its proper form.

I doubt we will cancel the myths of blind love any time soon because it feeds into the narrative that love is something that just happens to us beyond our control. Regardless of that lie, we have full control over who we love. Science is not saying that we don't have control. Rather, it is proving that we have the ability to allow ourselves to see the full picture if we so choose. Each day, my strong disdain for the phrase "love is blind" swells because it renders us powerless when, in reality, we have full power over with whom we choose to fall in love.

What am I saying here? Do not give your power to someone simply because you want to be in love so badly that you uphold a myth that does not and will not serve your ultimate goal: to find true love by seeing your partner's great characteristics as well as their flaws. By doing so, you take control in an effort to determine whether or not you want to move forward with this person, rather than feeling powerless, thinking, "I'm so in love I can barely see the realities of this person." Or, in hindsight, saying, "I saw that coming. I just ignored all the signs."

Now that we have a clear understanding of blind love from a cultural and psychological standpoint, let's examine what the brain is actually doing when we fall for someone. Because this is where the story gets interesting. The blind love question has a simple answer: yes and no. But what love actually does to your brain? That answer is far more useful to you.

Dopamine and Oxytocin: The Love Drugs

Prior to the 20th century, people generally believed that love was simply an emotion, albeit an overwhelming one. It seems our ancestors felt the same giddy, anxious feelings we do when we see someone we love. Our heart beats faster, thumping at a more discernible tempo. Our cheeks redden, our hands are clammy, butterflies swell in our stomachs, a big smile widens across our faces.

Today, we know that the heart's job is to pump blood to our extremities, and it seems we can feel each pump's vibration when we see or think about our partner. But the heart is not what truly makes us fall in and out of love. Research shows that all of these crazy, absolutely haywire feelings and physical reactions are led by the brain and the chemicals released when we experience attraction and desire. Attraction and, subsequently, love are complex emotions involving the interaction of multiple neurotransmitters and hormones.

Dopamine is the primary chemical involved in the initial rush, pleasure, and excitement that accompanies love. While the initial stages of a romantic relationship are often characterized by feelings of excitement and pleasure, as the relationship progresses, the nature of the individuals' connection with one another changes. The deeper, longer-lasting bond that develops between you and those you love is mediated by the hormone **oxytocin**. To fully understand how the brain operates when we experience a romantic or sexual connection, we must explore the role of dopamine and oxytocin in the development of those relationships.

Dopamine is a powerful neurotransmitter involved in a variety of reactions and emotions. It plays a role in motivation, movement, focus, pleasure, and reward. Your brain releases dopamine in response to pleasurable experiences, and scientists theorize it plays a key, if not paramount, role in the initial stages of falling in love. When we first meet someone attractive, our brains release dopamine, causing feelings of intense pleasure and excitement. Your neurons signal to the nucleus accumbens, your brain's stimulus control center, which floods your brain with feelings of intense euphoria. Science proves this. One study took brain scans of participants looking at someone special to them versus someone with whom they're acquaintances. When presented with pictures of those they loved, participants' brains showed dopamine release in the caudate nucleus, the part of the brain responsible for detecting rewards, and the ventral tegmental region, the area most often associated with pleasure and motivation.

The initial rush of dopamine is referred to as the relationship's honeymoon phase, characterized by feelings of happiness, anticipation, and desire. We become subsequently obsessed, or even addicted, during this process. It is within these early stages that your brain signals to your adrenal gland that there is a crisis, and we go into fight or flight mode. Over time, as dopamine levels increase, the body begins releasing cortisol, otherwise referred to as the stress hormone. As cortisol levels increase, serotonin levels lower, and low levels of serotonin cause the intrusive thoughts, fears, and desires that accompany a crush. If you're wondering why you bite your fingernails and find yourself wondering "do they like me" in a love struck panic, this is your answer.

Furthermore, the neurochemical processes that accompany early states of love effectively deactivate the amygdala, the brain's integrative control center. The amygdala is responsible for anxiety, anger, and sadness, as well as judgment and fear. While this occurs, the brain's frontal cortex becomes dampened. We lose our ability to think logically or with any degree of clarity. That's why you put up with people who are rude to waitstaff and chronically forget your anniversary. Our dampened judgment is why you ignored your shitty ex's red flags, as glaring as they were. When this process occurs, we falsely believe the other person can do no wrong.

As the relationship further progresses, dopamine releases become less frequent and, even worse, less intense, eventually leading to personal confusion. You might ask yourself, "Why don't I get excited like I used to? Things aren't as pleasurable as they used to be!" I've coached plenty of couples who experienced this at the one-year mark in their relationship, and my response is overwhelmingly the same: this isn't the end. Rather, it's a settling-in stage. Studies have been conducted to elucidate this phenomenon. It seems that over time, romanticism between couples declines, especially as the relationship becomes more committed. However, this does not mean relationships become stale. Instead, the initial rush of emotion, those nervous feelings in the pit of your stomach, subside, leaving mutual trust and contentment in their wake.

Dopamine isn't the only neurotransmitter involved in romantic relationships. Dopamine's role may be supplemented or replaced by other neurochemical pathways throughout the relationship's development. This brings us to oxytocin.

Oxytocin is a hormone produced in the hypothalamus, the organ responsible for regulating your body's subconscious processes, and is released by the pituitary gland, often referred to as the master gland because it regulates various hormonal activities throughout the body. Oxytocin is released in response to physical touch, intimacy, and certain social interactions. It is often coined the love hormone due to its theorized role in social bonding, attachment, calmness, and trust within close relationships. One study found that couples who were in long-term, monogamous relationships had higher levels of oxytocin in their blood than those who were single or in casual relationships, suggesting that oxytocin may play a role in the development of deeper, longer-lasting bonds between romantic partners.

Over time, people in love experience a dopamine connection, then an oxytocin connection. It's a direct process. While the initial pleasurable rush one feels when falling in love is dopamine-driven, the connection between individuals shifts toward a more stable, long-term bond as a result of oxytocin release over time. As the couple engages in physical and emotional intimacy, social interactions, and other bonding activities, their brains release more oxytocin, leading to increased feelings of attachment and commitment. This shift from a dopamine connection to an oxytocin connection can be gradual and may involve a number of other neurochemical pathways.

But does dopamine wear off? It will, eventually. Scientists theorize that over time, passionate love becomes what they call compassionate love, or love that is not quite as penetrating or euphoric but based on respect and commitment. This shift isn't boring or emotionless. Instead, love becomes more controllable and realistic as opposed to euphoric and haphazard. However, that doesn't mean you won't scratch your head at the six-month or one-year mark, thinking, "I just don't feel like I used to." When this happens, it's called settling in. The relationship has cadence and rhythm. Many people confuse this with being boring, but it's far from it.

Plainly speaking, oxytocin is responsible for long-term emotional connection and attachment, while dopamine release is immediate and responsible for short-term feelings of pleasure and euphoria. During the honeymoon stage, love acts like a drug and dopamine levels increase, making you feel happy and giddy. But as you get more comfortable with your partner, as you get to know them, and as the dopamine rush slowly wears off, these giddy feelings subside, ultimately testing the strength and foundation of the relationship.

Here is what the neuroscience is actually explaining when it maps the chemistry of attraction.

Chemistry is not random. It follows a pattern — your pattern. The nervous system does not simply respond to physical attractiveness. It responds to familiarity. And familiarity is built from the earliest relational environments you inhabited. The same environments that built your blueprint.

The Rescuer is chemically drawn to people who need something. The pull feels like love. It reads like a purpose. What it is, at the neurological level, is recognition, the body identifying a relational configuration it already knows how to inhabit.

The Skeptic is drawn to people who feel slightly out of reach. Not because unavailability is attractive in theory. Because the nervous system reads the chase as proof that something is worth wanting.

The Reactor is drawn to intensity. The emotional volume of early attraction mirrors what love felt like growing up which means lower intensity reads as disinterest, regardless of what the other person is actually offering.

The Escapist is drawn to people who feel safe specifically, people who will not demand more than the Escapist is prepared to give. That pull feels like ease. What it is, is a nervous system finding the configuration that allows it to stay close without having to stay fully present.

Chemistry feels like fate. Often it is just your pattern recognizing itself.

Here's where I want to push back on something you'll commonly hear, even in professional settings. Many therapists urge couples to get back to the feelings and activities that brought them together in the first place. I understand the intention behind this, but the science doesn't support it as a primary strategy. When people start dating, dopamine takes over, meaning that their feelings in the beginning aren't entirely their own anymore. We evolve as people, and that is perfectly natural. Because of this, how we see our partners one to five years into a relationship is quite different from how we saw them on the first date. The reconnection process should not be based on or replicated from the infancy stage of a relationship. Some couples were teenagers or young adults when they began dating. It would be unrealistic to tell two people in their forties to recreate the early experiences of a relationship they entered as entirely different people.

The Brain in Love

four chemicals that run the whole show

01 – REWARD

Dopamine

what it is

The brain's reward signal — released in the ventral tegmental area when something good is coming.

what it does

Drives motivation, craving, and pursuit. It fires before reward arrives — that's why wanting feels so urgent.

in love

That relentless need to see them again. The high of a new text. Obsessively replaying every moment.

02 – AROUSAL

Norepinephrine

what it is

Both a hormone and neurotransmitter — a chemical cousin of adrenaline, released under intense attention.

what it does

Raises heart rate, dilates pupils, cuts appetite. Sharpens your focus to a single point of interest.

in love

Sweaty palms. A racing heart. Can't eat. Can't sleep. The world narrows to one person.

03 – MOOD

Serotonin

what it is

A mood-regulating neurotransmitter made from tryptophan — most of it lives in the gut, not the brain.

what it does

High levels = calm and contentment. Low levels = rumination, compulsion, intrusive thoughts.

in love

Early love drops serotonin — which is why new love feels more like obsession than peace.

04 – BONDING

Oxytocin

what it is

A neuropeptide made in the hypothalamus — surges during touch, eye contact, and physical intimacy.

what it does

Builds trust, reduces anxiety, promotes empathy. Lowers cortisol. Makes you feel safe with one specific person.

in love

The warmth of skin-on-skin. The grief of separation. Oxytocin turns attraction into attachment.

← early attraction dopamine + norepinephrine dominate serotonin drops · oxytocin deepens lasting bond →

These chemicals don't work in isolation — they overlap, amplify, and sometimes compete.

Trauma Bonds

"We are bound by everything we've been through, and breaking away from him is like tearing flesh." — Celeste, *Big Little Lies*

Callie and Ryan came to me a few years ago when their relationship hit rock bottom. Ryan, a white man in his fifties, was an IT executive. His partner, Callie, in her late thirties, was a Black woman who worked in project management. When they came to me, they'd been together for less than three years but had moved in together only six months after they began dating. Most of their relationship was a whirlwind by anyone's standards. They'd entered into a committed relationship very shortly after their first date, got pregnant quickly, and married that same year. Two years after that, they welcomed their second child.

Nevertheless, they came to me to help them work through their gaps and issues, which, as I quickly deduced, were really traumas. As a couples coach, I have three sources of information that I draw from: what the partners report about themselves and each other, how they behave in front of me, and how I feel witnessing their behavior together. As I used these sources, I saw Ryan dodging questions, noticeably uncomfortable, crossing his arms, avoiding eye contact, and correcting both Callie and me, even when what we were saying wasn't in need of correction. Clarification was what he'd called it.

At one point, I asked him, "Did Callie force you into coming to this coaching session?" Ryan knew better than to lie. At work, he twisted himself into knots to please those around him, especially his superiors. At the time, Ryan was working over eighty hours a week and had little time for Callie and the kids.

"Not exactly," he replied. "But she certainly strongly suggested it." Ryan didn't necessarily believe there was anything wrong with the relationship. I could sense how much he cared for her. He loved how assertive Callie was and was physically attracted to her.

Like many of the clients I encounter, Ryan presented with child ego states in a transactional analysis called Adaptive Child, accompanied with Grandiosity. The former term refers to a child who was hurt by abuse or neglect whose characteristics developed as they learned to change their feelings and behaviors in response to the world around them. In adulthood, this helps them cope with their relational wounds but also brings dysfunction to their relationships. It is a later developing child who lives in past-time and cares only about self-protection, unwilling and unable to learn new skills. Simply put, it's an adult version of a child, one that developed in reaction to and resistance against its wounds in order to cope.

The latter term refers to someone obsessed with self-perception. Ryan was perfectionistic, rigid, unrealistic, and ultimately unforgiving. Ryan had grown up in a closely-knit alcoholic family without unconditional love. He learned to perform to earn their affection. As a child, he lacked attention, and his parents relied on him to take care of his siblings. More poignantly, they expected him to take care of their emotional and physical needs. His mindset contributed to his professional success but threatened to devastate his personal life, especially his relationship. Culture at large feeds off of Adaptive Children because as adults, they are highly agreeable and will do almost anything to gain attention and perceived love. As a child, Ryan learned to lie, not for malicious reasons, but so as not to anger his parents. So when I encountered his half-truths, I thought his upbringing might be a part of the issue. Upon thorough consideration, I thought, "Maybe, but perhaps there's more to it." As we worked together, Ryan showed me how he handled himself and his relational stance.

"Have you tried to stop lying on your own?" I asked him.

"Well I've tried, of course, but then again…" he began.

"What do you mean by try exactly?" I asked. He didn't know how to reply. Nevertheless, I continued. "Have you been struggling a long time?"

"I can't say I struggle per se…"

"You do struggle," Callie interjected. "You just don't admit it. You don't admit much of anything." She rolled her eyes.

"Cal…" he paused. "I do, it's just…"

"What?" she asked, leaning back in the chair. "Just what?"

After witnessing their exchange a few times, I began to see the full picture. Ryan would later tell me that he lied to stay out of trouble, and Callie, who was sitting next to him, let out a long exhale. If looks could kill, Ryan would have been dead in my office.

"Stay out of trouble?" she screamed, and once again rolled her eyes after a long exhale. "What does that even mean? You're acting like I'm your mother."

Over time, I began to understand the inner workings of their relationship. The two weren't compatible, at all, but they'd been deeply physically attracted to one another, at least at the beginning. Later in the chapter, I'll share with you why romantic chemistry isn't always a good thing. Callie had grown up in an impoverished household, one riddled with emotional and physical abuse, so when she met Ryan, she latched onto him, falling for his stability. Do you know what that's called? An emotional trauma bond and a hero-savior complex.

I decided to meet with each of them one-on-one. Ryan didn't budge during his individual sessions, remaining reserved, even cold at times. But Callie, on the other hand, was more forthright.

"I just don't think this is working," she told me one day.

"What's not working?" I asked. I knew the answer, but I needed her to say it out loud.

"Ryan and I," she murmured. "I'm bored. I take care of the kids, do his laundry, pick them up from preschool." She paused. "I had a whole life before this."

"Well," I began. "Why did you love him in the beginning?"

"He was kind and loving. He was everything I needed, I think. And I was super attracted to him."

I sighed. Callie confided in me that they'd met during one of the lowest points in her life. She'd lost a high six-figure job, was working through some residual emotional childhood trauma, and had a virtually nonexistent support system. She told me that Ryan was her hero. He was much older, financially stable, maintained an established career, and understood her emotionally. He provided stability, which was what she'd needed at that time.

"Did you think he'd heal you?" I asked her. Her face dropped.

"In a way, maybe." She crossed her legs. "I went to a therapist, by myself. They helped me work through some of my past, but since then, I've been feeling like I don't need him anymore."

Callie's trauma was deep and troubling. She told me she thought she was losing her mind at one point. Callie began healing from her past about eighteen months into the relationship, and at that time, she began to see Ryan and the relationship's flaws. In a way, she suddenly woke up, realizing she no longer wanted or needed this man or this marriage. When she came to this realization, she detached almost immediately, feeling trapped because of the kids. She'd come to hate everything about him: how he dressed, his scent, his haircut, and even the rotten tooth on the upper left side of his mouth.

"Why don't you need him?" I asked. Again, I knew the answer, but she needed to say it.

"I did it myself. I healed myself," she replied. "He's just not what I need anymore. Is that okay? Is that normal? I'm realizing that getting into a relationship with him was a mistake. It was out of my pain. I think I was acting out."

Ryan just wasn't the man for her. He was rigid, unforgiving, perfectionistic, and passive-aggressive. Callie was everything but. She was assertive, direct, and exceedingly compassionate. I think she cared for him deeply, but she didn't love him. I think that, at that time, she was incapable of loving anyone.

The two separated after nine years, but Ryan remained completely in love with her. His perfectionist, unwavering beliefs prevented him from understanding what happened or why the relationship failed. The two divorced a few years after their separation. Ryan had believed that his love for her would override her disdain for him. He didn't think he was the problem. I remember in one of our sessions, he said, "I think she's batshit crazy. I mean, look at me. She's lost her mind."

He, like most of us, fails to comprehend that love does not make relationships work. Love is what keeps the relationship moving.

At the end of Callie's and my last individual session, I asked, "Have you heard the term trauma bond?"

She nodded. "But this isn't that. It wasn't that. It was just… he was what I needed." After she said that, I kept quiet. I wanted the silence to fill the room. And after about two to three full minutes of silence, she blurted out, "OH SHIT, IT WAS A TRAUMA BOND!" As she was enlightened, tears began to roll down her cheeks. I thought, this is the perfect opportunity to dig deeper in such a way that would prevent her from ever finding herself in a situation like this again.

"He was what you needed because of your trauma, and because of his own. He's inclined to save people because it makes him feel needed. That's where his trauma manifests. That's what a trauma bond is. And you needed safety from the emotional and physically abusive family and romantic relationships you'd come to know." In a trauma-bonded relationship, we aren't loved for who we are. We are loved because of what we went through. That, in and of itself, is not true love.

Callie nodded again. "I think you're right," she said.

What happened between Callie and Ryan was not a failure of love. Love was present. What was absent was the foundation love requires to hold.

Callie came into the relationship running a blueprint shaped by poverty, abuse, and the absence of consistent safety. Ryan came in running a blueprint shaped by a family that conditioned love to performance. She needed rescue. He needed to be needed. That is not compatibility. That is two patterns finding each other in the dark and calling it a match.

Trauma plays a significant role in shaping our lives and personal narratives, and variations in its impact and severity shape an individual's perception of reality. Trauma is, at its core, a response to pain. Pain, over time, interrupts ongoing thought and behavior from within affective-motivational environments, causing long-term emotional, behavioral, or, in some cases, physical deficits. Older generations have their own ideas when it comes to trauma, and often discount or undermine its effects. However, science has proven that the pain that breeds trauma is an inescapable fact of life, and that pain will emerge over other demands for attention.

Over time, trauma becomes a legitimate part of a person's identity, and the way they express this should not be stigmatized or deemed pathological. Think back to Callie and Ryan. Both individuals had past traumas that made it difficult for them to emotionally function and self-regulate. It is essential to recognize that the expression and narration through which trauma is portrayed and communicated may be subject to negative judgment. Just like Callie and Ryan, we are subconsciously compelled to repeat unresolved trauma in our intimate relationships because it is what we have become accustomed to. It's our go-to defense and what brings us comfort.

A traumatic bond, or a **trauma bond**, is an attachment formed between two people who unconsciously bond to each other based on shared trauma, ultimately leading to relational betrayal and heartbreak. These bonds may simply be an illusion of affection or an authentic feeling, but nevertheless, those who enter into a trauma-bonded relationship do so to help themselves deal with their isolation and feelings of despondency, and to protect their emotional stability. Studies show that shared pain or trauma promotes co-operation because of pain's well-demonstrated capacity to capture attention and focus awareness on the immediate painful event. In other words, pain can be a natural bonding experience between groups and, subsequently, two people. Trauma bonds operate on this principle.

Before we go further, it is necessary to draw further attention to the definition presented in the previous paragraph. Take a moment with it. The individuals who share trauma form highly codependent bonds based on emotional attachment, and this attachment is often bidirectional. Callie was a little confused when I mentioned a trauma bond, because her perception of the term had been heavily influenced by society's definition of it. Trauma bonding is not to be confused with the official definition of narcissistic abuse. We commonly hear of traumatic bonds as synonymous with narcissistic abuse within our adult relationships. While this is sometimes true, the reality is that trauma bonds do not begin in our adult lives. Instead, they are perpetuated during our adult lives.

During abusive childhoods, traumatic bonds are a learned product of intermittent positive and negative reinforcement. Children who are praised for something one day and punished for it the next begin to perceive their world as unpredictable and inconsistent. They learn that their environment is unsafe and the people in their lives are unreliable. This type of situation can condition a child to become traumatically bonded to abusive, negligent, and narcissistic parents, and later in life, to highly narcissistic or toxic partners. When narcissistic values are at play, a child is likely not learning or receiving unconditional love. Children reared in certain conditions tend to learn that acceptance is based on their performance, that validation is based on approval-seeking, and that love is conditional, just as Ryan did. Children raised with these expectations can become withdrawn, angry, or fearful of further betrayal. Because of this early conditioning, they may be at an increased vulnerability and predisposition to traumatic bonds in their adult relationships.

When two people with these trauma-bred commonalities come together, they become both agents of pain and agents of coping for one another. When Callie met Ryan, she was experiencing an emotional low as a result of unresolved, unacknowledged past trauma. Ryan, whose personality and disposition had been similarly influenced by a traumatic childhood, complemented her traumas and made her feel safe. We mistakenly expect shared trauma to translate into compatibility, assuming that because the other person hurts the same, they will also love us the same or in the way we need. This causes a vicious cycle of revictimization between individuals, ensuring that neither of them advances beyond the pain that binds them together.

Have you ever been in or witnessed a relationship where one minute the two people are madly in love and the next, they are sworn enemies? This is a push-pull attachment style. **Love bombing**, the sudden, intense attempt to create a "we" in a relationship through high praise and excessive flattery, is a key feature of this dynamic. **Blame-criticism**, the back-and-forth dance of harsh criticism and over-apologizing that reinforces the trauma bond, is another. **Gaslighting and manipulation**, often seen in trauma bonds, make victims question their reality and perception. **Loss of self**, the erosion of social connections due to changes in self-identity, follows closely behind. And then there is what I call **addiction to the cycle**: after a significant conflict, trauma-bonded couples may find themselves in a cool down or honeymoon period. During this moment of peace, the abuser might apologize and start the love bombing process all over again.

Ryan and Callie experienced gaslighting, loss of self, blame-criticism, and addiction to the cycle. Though it may not seem as though Ryan was gaslighting Callie in the traditional sense, his apathetic demeanor and refusal to admit fault were a form of manipulation. Callie lost herself throughout their relationship, contributing to their addictive bond. Ryan wasn't abusing Callie, but his subconscious, unresolved traumas, coupled with hers, were a recipe for disaster. Callie herself was similarly culpable in the relationship's demise. She engaged in blame-criticism, criticizing and condemning Ryan's haircut, tooth, and so on, but later over-apologizing and blaming herself for the relationship's issues. Callie, like many who participate in trauma-bonded relationships, was addicted to the cycle. She and Ryan were often in significant conflict, and this conflict was always followed by a calm after the storm. Callie loved this cycle and craved the excitement. Instability, as many would perceive it, was Callie's picture-perfect relationship.

If you've seen *Big Little Lies*, then you've seen the complex nature of a trauma bond play out on screen. On the outside, Celeste and Perry have a loving, picture-perfect relationship. However, on the inside, their partnership is riddled with violence and emotional and physical abuse. Celeste loves and is bonded to Perry despite the abuse she endures. In one episode, she vocalizes the reason why she can't leave, saying they are bound by everything they've been through, and that breaking away is like tearing flesh. That statement's resounding power leaves me awestruck. It speaks volumes to both the truth and power of traumatic bonds. Celeste and Perry are simply one example.

The key to understanding a trauma-bonding relationship is that it cannot be healthy. Why? Because the relationship is not equal. Oftentimes when people are trauma bonding, it may look and feel safe, but there is great inconsistency within the relationship, and this inconsistency can be extremely dysfunctional. In all cases, there is some form of manipulation involved.

Too often, we try to build healthy relationships on unstable foundations, seeking out those who share our wounds instead of those who can help us heal. Instead of finding comfort in shared pain, we should look for partners who inspire growth and support our journey to wholeness.

Trauma and Chemistry

In all likelihood, you've been exposed to trauma-bonded relationships in one way or another. Oftentimes, these toxic dynamics look like passionate, hot-and-cold, love-hate relationships. It feels so incredibly good to just click with a new person romantically. We crave it with all of our being. Conversation flows. Inside jokes flourish. With every little touch on the arm comes a growing excitement. Everything indicates forward momentum, and then, one day, maybe a few weeks or months in, something changes. It becomes clear that something has been unclicked. Let me explain in detail why this is a harrowing issue.

Trauma is the lasting emotional response that often results from living through or being affected by a distressing event. In simpler terms, trauma is anything that impacts you negatively and leaves an emotional wound. The issue is this: the traumas each of us carry can be easily recreated within our relationships. This is why I caution against the notion that chemistry is everything. Don't be fooled by the instantaneous sparks. Chemistry isn't always a good thing.

When we are attracted to someone who lights up our internal wounds, we are pulled into a sort of dance. Most people in trauma-bonded relationships feel as though they're never bored, and this draws them to the other person. Chemistry can be deceptive. Two people can light up each other's emotional wounds and reenact all of their childhood traumas, as Callie and Ryan did. And the worst part is, these reenactments can feel exciting. The emotional whirlwind of landing the unbelievable guy or the wild woman keeps the vicious cycle going.

I'm about to tell you something that is going to be uncomfortable. If you're constantly seeking thrilling relationships, it is possible you are actually seeking a person who will light up your trauma wounds.

These relationships can feel like a thrilling roller coaster ride, the kind you look forward to the minute you step foot into the theme park. The problem with a roller coaster ride is that once you're on, it is nearly impossible to hop off while it's racing down the track. We leave the ride disheveled, dizzy, and confused. If we are used to this dynamic in relationships, we view it as normal. But in reality, this dynamic isn't normal. Far from it.

The nice guy or girl might seem boring, but don't let that fool you. In this sense, boring is a good thing. When you're used to trauma and its highs and lows, you might reject stability. The word boring comes with a negative connotation, but it's anything but. There is inherent peace in stability. If you're on a roller coaster ride that never affords you the opportunity to hop off and have your needs met, you will stay stuck in this vicious cycle. And at that point, is it really worth the thrill? You wouldn't get in a car with a drunk driver. Why? Because you fear bodily harm. So why are you still in that toxic relationship? It is similarly causing you damage, emotionally. At what point are you going to get out of the car, stop hitting walls, and stop crashing into trauma?

My suggestion to you is simple. Take a deeper look into what is truly being recreated on this roller coaster ride, and find the real reason why you crave intensity and thrill. You can still find a true, healthy connection with another person that provides thrills through genuine understanding without trauma's baggage. To be clear, everyone has some sort of trauma. I'm speaking about those who refuse to deal with their trauma, ultimately pretending it doesn't exist.

Stop Mistaking Shared Trauma for Compatibility

Shared pain brings people together. That much is true. Many studies focusing on pain in a social context corroborate this statement. In fact, some studies show pain's bonding capacity not only operates in situations where individuals experience a certain degree of pain at the same time but that merely sharing painful experiences with other people promotes cooperation.

From a sociological standpoint, evolved responses to pain serve to generate social support from others, ultimately bonding us to those who share with us their experience. Known to sociologists as social glue, trauma, which in this context is pain's sequel, behaves like a binding agent in social settings, forging connections between survivors. These connections are, similarly, trauma bonds.

We are inherently attracted to those who share experiences with us. In general, individuals prefer partners with a similar attachment style, or complementary attachment style, especially in the early stages of a relationship. Hence why Callie and Ryan entered a serious relationship so quickly. Their attachment styles mirrored one another's. However, studies show that we're attracted to those who mirror us on another level entirely. One study concluded that secure individuals prefer similarly secure partners, and it may be deduced that the opposite is similarly true. This does not mean partners are compatible. This is a cultural misconception. Just because two people experienced a similar childhood or share a traumatic background does not mean they are going to waltz into the sunset. These relationships rarely, if ever, end with three kids, grandchildren, and a house in the suburbs. They're a recipe for disaster.

I would be doing you a disservice if I didn't give you the full picture in the context of relationships in general, including platonic ones. Compatibility as it intersects with trauma bonding is not limited to romantic relationships. For some people, friendship trauma bonding involves speaking their truths together and becoming friends through a deeply layered experience. This experience can be deeply empathetic, heavy, eye-opening, perspective-providing, and emotionally arousing all at once. It is the act of saying: This is who I am. This is how I am who I am. This is what I am afraid of becoming. This is who I have become despite and because of fear. This is how I have survived. Friendships are relationships, and therefore trauma-bonded friendships are similarly prevalent. Studies looking at war veterans find that heavy combat veterans are more likely than other veterans to have enduring ties. There is nothing explicitly wrong with being honest, of course, but we must acknowledge the effect of trauma on all of our relationships, not simply those that are romantic. So if you see any of these patterns in your own friendships, pay attention.

Similarities Bond but Differences Build

Let us not confuse trauma bonds with similarities between two people. Intimate relationships, romantic or not, are complex and multifaceted, encompassing a wide range of emotions, behaviors, and personal or shared experiences. While no two intimate relationships are entirely alike, there are certain key elements common within successful, healthy relationships. One such element is the interplay between similarities and differences within a committed relationship.

Contrary to popular belief, I strongly believe, and have seen plenty of evidence, that similarities bond but differences build. Let me clarify. While our compatibility helps us bond to our partners, it is our differences that build our relationships. It is easy to find commonalities and use those to bond to others, but that leaves us with a different challenge: how can we overcome the differences between us and our partner in order to make a relationship work? Ultimately, if we're able to overcome our differences, it is these differences that become the building blocks to a successful and healthy relationship.

Similarities, such as shared values, interests, goals, personality traits, communication styles, and intimacy preferences, provide a foundation of mutual comfort and understanding that creates a strong, lasting bond between partners. These similarities allow partners to feel connected and understood, providing a sense of common purpose that sustains the relationship long-term. Additionally, similarities can provide a source of shared meaning and motivation, helping partners to work together toward common goals.

At the same time, differences derived from various sources play a significant role in the development and dynamics of our relationships. Differences in perspective, values, life experiences, personality, communication styles, and intimacy preferences can bring new ideas and experiences into the relationship, helping keep things fresh and exciting, especially in the bedroom. Additionally, differences provide opportunities for growth, learning, and exploration, allowing partners to understand and appreciate each other's unique needs and desires. However, in some cases, differences in the aforementioned areas can become a source of tension and conflict.

It is important to acknowledge that differences are a natural facet of any relationship and should be viewed as opportunities to learn, not as threats to the relationship. By embracing and valuing these differences, partners build a relationship that is both strong and resilient, while strengthening their ability to weather challenges and grow together over time. To embrace these differences, we must acknowledge that our partner is a unique collection of personal experiences and dispositions, and these dispositions inherently affect the relationship.

As we discussed earlier in the chapter, certain neurological pathways and chemical reactions play a role in the disillusionment many couples experience near the beginning of their relationship. We see what we want to see. We ignore red flags, potential issues, and differences, choosing to focus on the person's more favorable qualities. As the relationship progresses, we must come to grips with reality and acknowledge that personal dispositions are ingrained in genetics and reinforced by early experiences and attachment bonds. It boils down to respect. Respect is among the most important underpinnings in any relationship, platonic or romantic. Yet, if approached in a positive and constructive way, differences can be a source of growth and learning for both partners.

One of the key ways that differences can positively cultivate and improve a relationship's dynamic is through creating shared diverse experiences and perspectives. This diversity helps each partner view the world in new, novel ways, ultimately providing them with opportunities for personal growth and learning. One partner may have a different background, culture, or set of experiences, which brings new and fresh perspectives to the relationship. Their background or personal experiences might at some point create tension. They might be used to a certain type of cuisine, they don't enjoy loud music because of certain past traumas, or they enjoy something a little kinky in the bedroom. Their proclivities might annoy the other person at first, or they might not understand them, but if the two listen and communicate, they might find they love their partner's homemade Feijoada. By embracing and valuing these differences, partners gain a deeper appreciation for each other and for the world around them. This is one of the reasons why I am a cheerleader for interracial and intercultural relationships.

Another way differences can shape the dynamics of intimate relationships is through the creation of new challenges, and these challenges similarly lead to new growth opportunities for the individuals involved. Partners may have different levels of comfort regarding emotional intimacy, leading to differences in communication styles and intimacy preferences. When couples understand and appreciate these differences, they work together, deepening their intimacy and finding new ways to meet each other's needs. Altogether, this teamwork leads to greater intimacy and connection within the relationship.

When partners recognize the importance of differences, they have the opportunity to create a dynamic, exciting, constantly evolving relationship that provides each individual the opportunity to grow, learn, and explore their inner motivations and ideologies.

As detailed above, love is a chemical reaction governed by neurological pathways that trigger emotional responses. During the early stages of a relationship, these reactions effectively blind us to a partner's reality, making us unaware of their proclivities, negative habits, and possible red flags. Trauma bonds exacerbate the problem. Those who have unresolved trauma are inherently attracted to those who can lick their wounds, and falsely assume that because the other person has lived a difficult life or shares similar traumatic past experiences, they can heal us. This is far from the case. Love is developed by both shared characteristics and differences, and it is these differences that cultivate personal growth for couples, allowing them to, in turn, gain trust in the relationship. Love itself isn't blind. It blinds us. And to regain sight, we must see the other person for who they are, celebrate what makes them, and communicate to develop the relationship.

Exercise: The Attraction Pattern Audit:
https://go.carloshines.com/book/attraction-audit
or Scan the QR Code below

The Comparison Trap

Social media has an inescapable presence in our daily lives today, with platforms such as Facebook, Instagram, TikTok, and Twitter boasting billions of users. Everyone uses social media a bit differently, but for the most part, users use these platforms to consume entertainment, connect with friends and family, and share their experiences with others. We spend a great deal of time on social media. The global average, as of now, is two hours and forty-one minutes a day. Over a lifetime, this equates to six years and eight months of our lives spent scrolling.

Additionally, newer scientific studies examining our use of social media illuminate its addictive qualities and conclude that addictive social media use is associated with negative consequences such as reduced productivity, unhealthy social relationships, and reduced life satisfaction. There are many reasons why this is the case. Prominent psychologists believe it is due to widespread feelings of loneliness and isolation, and sociologists build on this theory, believing we have a strong need to feel connected without actually maintaining the desire to connect. Tech companies intentionally build algorithms to keep us entertained, even addicted, to our phones. Our growing reliance on social media raises serious concerns about its impact on relationships, especially romantic ones. We know the problem exists. Just look around. Everyone is on their phone regardless of the social setting. But many of us do not know how to navigate it. I want to expound on why couples focus more on social media than on each other, and discuss its long-term consequences on a relationship.

Harper and Madison came to me a while ago to fix their relationship, as if I were a genie in a bottle. Immediately, I explained to both of them that there is no magic in fixing a relationship. It involves hard work and commitment, not magic. Harper and Madison were a young couple in their twenties, and both identified as bisexual. I quickly recognized within each of them a gravitation to immediacy, an obsession with what was in front of them, which was reflected in the way they approached their relationship.

Our second session was the turning point, my aha moment, so to speak. The two arrived separately. Madison from work, and Harper from an outing with friends, or so they explained. Madison arrived first and, before saying a word, pulled out her phone. I was stunned by how much they were obsessed with their phones, even in our sessions.

"Something for work?" I asked her, though, from her phone's reflection on the picture frame behind her, I could see she was on TikTok.

She looked up at me for a moment and crossed her legs. "You could say that," she said with a small laugh. Harper arrived shortly after, phone in hand.

When her phone buzzed, Madison would jump. When Harper's dinged, he unconsciously reached down to grab it before correcting himself, even amid conversation. If they can't stay off their phones in talk therapy, how on earth do they stay off their phones when they're hanging out at home? I thought. The answer was simple: they didn't.

So I asked, "Do you two do anything without a phone in hand?" They looked at one another, a little confused.

"No," Harper mumbled, leaning back into his seat. Madison looked at him and rolled her eyes, not enough for Harper to notice, but just enough for me.

"What do you two do when you spend time together?" They looked at each other once more, even more confused. Madison knew what I was getting at, but Harper seemed out of the loop. "We hang out," Madison said, looking out the window, not at me.

"Do you leave the phones at home?" I asked. They didn't shake their heads, but neither nodded. "Or, at the very least, turn them off?" Madison, always quick to justify, shook her head in annoyance. "We have to check on things."

As a relationship expert with over 15 years of experience working with couples, I know that most issues within relationships arise from traumas or learned behaviors. I can also tell with 85% accuracy, within the first twenty minutes of observing and interacting with a couple, whether or not they will have a healthy relationship. I had high hopes for this couple but knew they weren't willing to give up their bad habits or do the work to repair what they'd broken.

During an individual session with Madison, she kept her phone in her bag, but it buzzed relentlessly. This is the very reason why I no longer allow cell phones in sessions.

"Is there an emergency?" I asked, just innocuously enough so as not to sound intrusive.

"It's a friend," she replied shortly. I assured Madison our meetings were confidential, and she finally confided in me that she was talking to someone she'd met just before she and Harper made their relationship official. When I asked her if her new fling was physical, her face dropped like she'd been caught in a horrible lie.

"Not yet," she muttered.

"Will it be? Eventually?" I asked her, looking at her knowingly.

"If I'm being honest..."

"Please do," I interjected.

"Yes," she told me. Madison was a journalist who'd found a platform on social media. She made engaging TikToks and had amassed thousands of followers who loved her honesty. Madison later revealed to me that she didn't feel seen. She felt like Harper wasn't paying attention to her. She still cared for Harper and found him attractive, very much so, she assured me, but wasn't getting what she needed.

My sessions with Harper were similarly revealing. His arm reached down to his phone every time it lit up. At another session, I asked what he did online, what he was so completely preoccupied with. "I just look at things," he murmured.

"What are these things?" I asked. "How do they make you feel?"

"I just..." he stuttered. "I don't like being on my phone, but I don't want to miss anything. I feel worse about it at night. But during the day, it feels like a necessity."

"What makes you feel worse about it at night?" I asked.

"I get lonely," he told me. "It gives me something to look forward to."

"And Madison doesn't?" I asked.

Harper didn't say anything, but he didn't have to. Madison wasn't contributing to his happiness.

Both partners were struggling to separate themselves from social media and the immediate satisfaction it provides. Madison didn't feel she was receiving adequate attention from Harper, so she indulged in social media and gained validation from the likes she received when she posted photos. She began to emotionally check out of the relationship, and her behavior was inching toward infidelity. Harper was a little different. He explained to me that he felt pressured to maintain the relationship and overcompensated, bringing her flowers, calling her often, and texting her hourly. He'd noticed Madison pulling away and began retreating online himself. Both ignored the real issues within the relationship, and cracks began to form. One partner pushed forward while the other pulled away. It became a cycle neither of them knew how to stop.

After our third session, I realized the two of them had nothing in common. Harper was driven, dedicated, and a little perfectionistic. He'd never let anyone know he wasn't okay, hated admitting fault, and didn't seem to mind living in the background. Madison, in contrast, valued appearances. She spent hours at the gym each week and was nearing credit card debt. I suggested a 30-day break from sex to help them clear their heads and rationalize their bond, and it was this break that revealed to both of them that they had nothing to bond over except for sex. It seemed sex was the only thing keeping them together, and Madison ended the relationship on day sixteen.

What Harper and Madison could not name, they could not interrupt. Harper was running a Rescuer pattern in full activation: overcompensating, calling hourly, bringing flowers, trying to earn his way back into a connection that was already closing. Madison was running an Escapist response: seeking external validation because internal presence had become too costly, retreating toward distance while staying technically in place.

Neither of them was broken. Both of them were patterned. And neither had language for what was actually happening. So it looked like incompatibility. It looked like two people who were simply wrong for each other.

Sometimes that is true. But more often, it is just two patterns running without interruption. This is what that looks like.

Romantic Consumerism

Our reliance on social media represents a relatively new cultural phenomenon, one that remains underexplored and under-discussed, and it has given rise to something I want to name directly: **romantic consumerism**.

Romantic consumerism is an ideology that promotes the notion that love and romance can be commodified, that we enter relationships the way we enter a store, with a list of what we want and an expectation of what we're entitled to receive. We are never fully satisfied with that list, so we keep adding to it, wanting more and more each time. As much as we may not care to admit it, we begin going out of our way to collect as many experiences and partners as possible. Basically, we're saying, "I'm shopping for something, and I have a list of what it needs to be."

When we enter a romantic experience, we seek to take our partner's positive qualities, mannerisms, and personal traits and utilize them in our next relationship, adopting a capitalistic, consumerist view of romantic connection. But we are not willing to give more in return. It's just like shopping at the dollar store: we want quality products but only wish to pay five dollars or below for them. In reality, you get what you pay for. It doesn't make sense to expect a high-quality, functioning product for a two-dollar price tag, and more so, it doesn't make sense to become upset when that product does not meet your standards. Madison was clearly with Harper to fulfill a personal need for validation, and, in some way, Harper did the same. The two felt the need to sample one another and fell into the early relationship dopamine trap.

In short, romantic consumerism causes us to feel we must sample various kinds of relationships. It is characterized by a focus on short-term, superficial connections, ultimately signifying our preoccupation with novelty and excitement as opposed to long-term, stable commitment and emotional connection. And because we are never satisfied, we choose to keep shopping.

This idea was not present within our culture a century ago, but today, we're obsessed with defining ourselves and romanticizing an idealized image, not of who we are, but of who we'd like to be. We see this phenomenon in reality TV shows that feature wealthy protagonists showering their partners with lavish gifts and tropical vacations. Shows like *The Bachelor, Love is Blind, The Perfect Match, Love Island*, and *Are You the One?* prey on our vulnerabilities while using love in such a consumeristic way that it makes me want to turn the television off entirely. These shows portray a love that causes society to think, "I should have twenty options of available partners at my disposal at any given moment." Dating apps and advertising only perpetuate this misconception by encouraging consumers to buy products that promise to enhance their romantic lives.

One of the most significant consequences of romantic consumerism is the rise of **serial monogamy**: the practice of engaging in a series of exclusive, committed relationships, one right after the other. Rather than staying committed to one partner long-term, those who practice serial monogamy find themselves in a vicious cycle of short-term relationships. Social media fast-tracks this process. We have access to an entire pool of potential partners at our fingertips, each representing the promise of a new, thrilling connection.

Because we hop from one relationship to the next, we do not give ourselves time to recalibrate. And recalibration matters. We give so much of ourselves in relationships that we need time to readjust, refocus on ourselves, and realign with who we are. Without that time, we pick up trauma from each relationship and drag it with us to the next one. That trauma doesn't always rear its head immediately. Sometimes it doesn't surface for months, if not years, down the road. But I promise you, it will.

Dragging around unprocessed relationship trauma is exhausting. It takes a toll on us physically, emotionally, and relationally. And over time, this exhaustion prevents individuals from developing the emotional skills necessary to build long-term, committed relationships. It contributes to widespread feelings of loneliness and dissatisfaction and, within the individual, may contribute to mental health issues such as anxiety and depression.

The bottom line is this: romantic consumerism is making it harder for all of us to love well. The antidote isn't giving up on relationships. It's learning to see them as something you build rather than something you consume.

It is worth naming what drives romantic consumerism at the individual level, because the cultural explanation only goes so far.

The person who keeps shopping rather than committing is not simply reflecting cultural conditioning. Often, they are running a Skeptic or Escapist blueprint underneath the behavior. The shopping is not really about finding a better option. It is about maintaining a safe enough distance from the vulnerability that real commitment requires. The consumerism is the pattern's most socially acceptable expression. It looks like high standards. What it is, is managed distance wearing the clothes of selectivity.

Appearances Versus Reality: Virtual Perfection Is Not Real-Life Perfection

As humans, we inherently crave social validation. Much of the internet, especially within the social media landscape, is designed to cater to this need. As a result, we feel a certain pressure to present the best of our lives: the graduations and medals, the promotions and accolades, the cute little things our partners do for us once in a blue moon, and images of us on vacations or during nights out. We do not post our failures or the tiny intrusive thoughts that keep us up at night. We desire validation, positive validation specifically, and we present content meant to solidify and substantiate what we perceive to be our worth.

Social media is bursting at the seams with images of seemingly perfect relationships, families, and lifestyles. These images cause us to compare our relationships and lives to those we see online, causing internal feelings of inadequacy and pervasive low self-esteem. Additionally, these images solidify unrealistic and often harmful expectations, creating standards that are difficult and often impossible to replicate within our offline lives. Like Harper, we feel dissatisfied in our day to day and look inward, thinking, "Why isn't my life and relationship perfect like this person's?"

Scientific studies support this claim. More frequent social media use has been associated with poorer psychological well-being, and over time and with repeated use, a user's self-worth becomes dependent on social media feedback. Those who repeatedly engage with technology report lower levels of self-satisfaction and more depressive and stress symptoms than their unplugged counterparts. Furthermore, users who suffer from low self-esteem are more likely to compensate by creating an idealized picture of themselves online, causing a cycle of emotional turmoil.

But it goes beyond the personal. Constant exposure to seemingly perfect relationships, lifestyles, and bodies through social media not only affects the individual. These feelings, in turn, cause pervasive feelings of inadequacy, insecurity, and anxiety within couples.

Here is how it plays out. Perhaps one partner in a couple is scrolling through TikTok and comes across an influencer duo. The couple appears young, happy, and healthy, posting about their perceived successes. The partner scrolls through their page for a while and begins feeling that their relationship cannot or does not compare. They reflect on last night's fight over the dishes or the baby crying in the bedroom and feel as though their life pales in comparison to the ones presented online. The partner might come across the couple's photos from their most recent vacation to the Maldives and look inwardly, feeling as though their own body is inadequate. They feel pressure to conform to these unrealistic standards, leading to envy, a distorted body concept, and low self-esteem.

And those feelings do not stay contained to the individual. They affect the relationship and are reflected in their interactions with their partner. The partner in question may begin to feel insecure about the quality of their relationship and their own life, leaving them both anxious and unhappy. This was Harper and Madison's downfall. Harper's time and attention online made Madison feel inadequately cared for and unattended to, causing her to escape to social media for validation and likes. Harper felt pressure to make the relationship better, looked online for ideas, and fell short. Compared to those he saw online, he felt inadequate. No good came out of it for either of them.

Individuals need to be mindful of the impact of social media on their perceptions of the word perfect and to limit exposure to idealized images to maintain healthy and happy offline relationships.

Social Media and Couples: A Breakdown

They say the first step to solving a problem is acknowledging its presence. Before we discuss possible solutions, let's discuss some of the specific ways social media pulls couples apart.

The Need for Social Validation: Social media platforms are a kind of stage, allowing individuals to showcase or perform certain moments of their lives and, in turn, seek validation from other users. This validation takes many forms: likes, comments, followers, friends, and shares. The instantaneous nature of this validation is addictive, leading to excessive use or even reliance on the platform.

In general, people present a polished version of their lives online, showing other users only the positives, none of life's negatives. This creates a sense of competition and social pressure to present an idealized version of oneself online. Those who seek this validation from their followers, in turn, spend more time on social media and less time with their partners, as Madison did in our example. The constant need for social validation is a relationship's poison, the symptoms of which are feelings of inadequacy, jealousy, and resentment.

The Fear of Missing Out: Social media makes it incredibly easy for its users to keep up with their friends and the latest moments in each other's lives. Constant exposure to immediate information causes a fear of missing out on what we perceive to be important events and key updates. Not only is this stressful and anxiety-inducing, but it is time-consuming. We cannot, nor should we, be expected to keep up with every ping and banner. When couples focus more on social media than on each other, the result is decreased quality time spent with one another, which ultimately threatens the relationship's communication and foundation.

The Availability of Distractions: Social media provides our minds with an endless supply of distractions, from scrolling through exponentially growing feeds to watching videos and playing engaging games. This consistent stream of distractions leads to decreased communication but also contributes to decreased intimacy between partners. This is when the water deepens. Now we are seeing a lack of satisfaction within a relationship and increased conflict as a result.

Attention and Time Diversion: Social media actively diverts precious time and attention away from our partners. People spend countless hours scrolling through their feeds, checking updates, and interacting with others. This time doesn't come from thin air. It is taken away from our partners. **Attention diversion** refers to the increased attention couples spend on social media rather than on each other, and is a key factor in modern relationship failures. **Time diversion** refers to the significant amount of time pulled away from one's partner and redirected toward social media. Furthermore, social media causes multitasking, as people are often checking their phones while also spending time with their partners, effectively reducing the quality of their interactions.

Over time, decreases in quality time and reductions in intimacy lead to a couple's loss of emotional connection, which is what binds us to one another in the first place. Attention and time diversion contributed to the weak bond between Harper and Madison. When Harper spent more time online, Madison followed suit to seek validation, leading to a nonexistent emotional connection between them.

Don't believe everything you see online. The emotional connections we believe we feel as a result of time on social media are a fallacy. You may think you know an influencer and feel a connection to them, but that person isn't real to you. They are a facade, and a convincing one.

Social media and its implications on our modern relationships form a cycle that negatively affects both our relationships and our quality of life. When we compulsively engage with social media, we inadvertently spend less time with our partners, ultimately decreasing the quality of our interactions, diminishing our emotional connection, and leaving both partners feeling unsatisfied. This dissatisfaction causes low intimacy, and by intimacy, I do not necessarily mean sex. I mean the late-night conversations, the hand-holding, the laying in bed discussing the future. Low intimacy leads to conflict, causing partners to spend more time idealizing other people they meet online and learning to prioritize these perfect relationships over the one they have right in front of them. It's a cycle, but it's one you can certainly stop.

Do you want to live your life in person with the one you love, or online drooling over a life and relationship that isn't yours? I choose the former. Every time.

Exercise: The Comparison Audit:
https://go.carloshines.com/book/comparison-audit
or Scan the QR Code below

You know where the patterns come from, the households, the hidden curriculum, the inherited models, the neuroscience of attraction, the cultural machinery that shapes what we believe love is supposed to look like and feel like and cost us. Six chapters of groundwork. Not to overwhelm you. To make sure that what comes next has something solid to land on.

What you need now is the name for what all of it built inside you.

Section II is where that happens. Phase 1 of the Re/Model Framework begins here. Remove the Gridlock. Find the pattern. Trace it to its source. Build the tools to interrupt it before it runs your next relationship the way it has run the ones behind you.

Everything in Section I was preparation. This is where the work starts.

II

Breaking the Pattern

*You are beginning Phase 1 of the Re/Model Framework™.
Remove the Gridlock. And the first act of removing gridlock is
this: finding the pattern that has been running your relationships
without your permission.*

What's Your Pattern?

Everything in Section II is Phase 1 work: finding the pattern, tracing the wound underneath it, understanding what drives it, and beginning to build the tools to interrupt it. You cannot recalibrate a connection while gridlock is still in place. And you cannot remove gridlock you have not yet named.

So we start here. With the name.

Take the Re/Model Pattern Assessment before continuing with the chapter. It's a short assessment tool that identifies your dominant pattern, names the specific fears driving it, and gives you a clear picture of how it's likely showing up in your relationships right now. It takes about five minutes and delivers the kind of clarity that most people spend years in therapy trying to arrive at.

**You can find it here: www.carloshines.com/quiz
or scan the QR Code at the end of the Introduction**

After years of working with couples and individuals, I began to notice something. Beneath the surface arguments about money, sex, communication, and trust, beneath all of it, there were recurring behavioral patterns. Not random ones. Not unique ones. The same four patterns, showing up again and again, across different backgrounds, different ages, different relationship structures. Four distinct ways that human beings protect themselves from the pain of intimate connection.

I call them the Four Relationship Patterns. And odds are, you're living inside one of them right now.

SIDEBAR: Your pattern isn't a personality flaw. It's a protection strategy that outlived its usefulness. The problem isn't that it doesn't work. It's that it works too well.

Why Patterns Form

Before we name the four patterns, let's be clear about where they come from.

We don't develop protective behavioral patterns in a vacuum. They are learned responses, forged in childhood, reinforced by experience, and calcified over years of repetition. When a child grows up in an environment where expressing needs leads to rejection, they learn to suppress those needs. When a teenager discovers that being helpful keeps the peace, they learn to over-function. When a young adult finds that getting louder is the only way to be heard, they learn to escalate. When someone is betrayed enough times, they learn to guard.

None of these are character defects. They are survival intelligence. At the time they were formed, they worked. They kept you emotionally safe. They helped you navigate unpredictable, sometimes dangerous relational environments. The brain is extraordinarily good at learning what keeps us alive, and in early relationships, emotional safety can feel just as life-or-death as physical safety.

The problem is that the nervous system doesn't automatically update its operating system when circumstances change. What protected you at nine is still running at thirty-four. The strategy that helped you survive a cold or chaotic household is the same strategy sabotaging your relationship today.

This is what I mean when I say you're patterned, not broken. The pattern isn't evidence of damage. It's evidence of adaptation. But adaptation that no longer serves you is just another word for stuck.

Read the four patterns below with that in mind. You're not looking for something to be ashamed of. You're looking for a mirror.

The Four Relationship Patterns

Pattern 1: The Escapist

The Escapist has learned, at a deep cellular level, that emotional proximity is dangerous. Not intellectually. They may fully believe in love, desire connection, and genuinely care about their partner. But somewhere in the architecture of their nervous system is an old lesson: closeness leads to pain, so distance leads to safety.

This shows up as withdrawal. The silent treatment that lasts days. The sudden need for space that appears right when the relationship starts to deepen. The chronic avoidance of hard conversations, not out of laziness but out of a body that physically braces for impact when vulnerability enters the room. The Escapist will often describe themselves as private or independent, and they are, but beneath that self-sufficiency is frequently a quiet ache for the closeness they keep pushing away.

Escapists often grew up in environments where emotional expression was met with criticism, dismissal, or unpredictability. They learned that going small, going quiet, was how you survived someone else's emotional volatility. Now, in adult relationships, their nervous system still reads emotional intensity as a threat, even when the threat is just love getting too real too fast.

The Escapist's greatest strength is their capacity for self-reflection and their ability to stay calm in a storm. But that same calm becomes a wall when their partner is standing on the other side of it, alone, wondering if they're loved at all.

The reframe: you didn't learn to disappear because you didn't care. You learned to disappear because no one ever taught you that staying wouldn't cost you everything.

SIDEBAR: If your default response to emotional intensity is to go quiet, go numb, or go somewhere else, physically or mentally, you may be operating from the Escapist pattern. Notice it. That's the first move.

Pattern 2: The Rescuer

The Rescuer is the one who holds everything together. They're the planner, the peacemaker, the emotional first responder. They show up when things fall apart. They fix what's broken. They give more than they receive, often voluntarily, often without being asked. And they do it all with a warm smile and what looks like an inexhaustible reserve of generosity.

Until they don't.

Because beneath the surface of the Rescuer's giving is an equation: if I am useful enough, I will be loved. If I stop being helpful, I will be abandoned. Their generosity is not always as unconditional as it appears. It is often a deeply unconscious transaction, a constant payment toward the relationship's emotional mortgage, driven by a terror that simply being themselves, without the service, will not be enough.

The Rescuer often grew up in a household where love was conditional on performance. Maybe they were the child who kept the peace between warring parents. Maybe they learned early that being needed was safer than being vulnerable. Maybe they were praised so consistently for their helpfulness that their identity became fused with it. Whatever the origin, the pattern is the same. They give and give until the resentment they never voiced accumulates into a wall no amount of giving can dismantle.

What makes this pattern particularly painful is that Rescuers are often deeply compassionate, incredibly loyal, and genuinely caring. But they have mistaken self-abandonment for love. They have confused over-functioning with partnership. And they will burn themselves completely out before they ever ask for what they actually need, because asking feels like failure, and failure feels like the beginning of the end.

The reframe: your care is one of the most beautiful things about you. But care without self-preservation is not love. It's a slow disappearance. You are not a resource. You are a person who deserves to be held, not just to hold.

SIDEBAR: Ask yourself: in my closest relationships, am I giving because I want to, or because I'm afraid of what happens if I don't? The honest answer will tell you everything.

Pattern 3: The Reactor

The Reactor feels everything at full volume. When they love, they love hard. When they hurt, they hurt loud. When conflict arrives, it doesn't simmer. It ignites. They are present, passionate, and emotionally alive in ways that can be magnetic and terrifying in equal measure.

The core wound of the Reactor is the fear of being unseen. Somewhere in their history, often in a household that was emotionally chaotic, dismissive, or inconsistent, they learned that the only way to register was to escalate. The quiet request went unheard. The polite complaint got dismissed. The tears were called dramatic. But the outburst? That got a response. It may not have been a good response, but it was a response, and to a nervous system desperate for proof that it exists and matters, any response beats silence.

This pattern creates a painful irony in adult relationships. The Reactor desperately wants connection, but their intensity frequently drives away the very people they're reaching toward. They push, the partner retreats. They escalate, the partner shuts down. Then the Reactor reads the shutdown as confirmation of their worst fear, that they are too much, that they will always be abandoned, and the cycle repeats.

After the storm passes, Reactors often feel profound remorse. They don't want to be the person who said that, who broke that thing, who made their partner flinch. But remorse alone doesn't interrupt the pattern. Without the tools to recognize the internal alarm that precedes the explosion and to respond differently to it, the regret becomes another component of the cycle rather than the beginning of the end of it.

The reframe: you are not too much. You were just in environments that were too small to hold you. Your passion is not the problem. It needs a different channel.

SIDEBAR: If you find yourself saying "I don't know why I said that" or "I didn't mean for it to go that far" more than once a month, the Reactor pattern is likely present. Intensity without strategy is just repetition.

Pattern 4: The Skeptic

The Skeptic has been burned. Maybe more than once. Maybe enough times that the fire no longer surprises them. They've simply learned to expect it. Where others enter relationships with hope, the Skeptic enters with one hand extended and the other one on the exit door. Not because they don't want love. Because they've stopped fully believing it's safe.

The Skeptic's most defining behavior is the test. Often unconscious, rarely acknowledged, but always present. They create small scenarios, intentionally or not, designed to find out if this person, too, will ultimately disappoint them. They pull back to see if their partner pursues. They withhold to see if they're noticed. They create friction to see if it ends things. In many cases, it eventually does, which the Skeptic then registers as evidence that they were right to be guarded in the first place.

This pattern tends to emerge from histories of betrayal, inconsistency, or relational unpredictability. The parent who promised one thing and delivered another. The partner who was faithful until they weren't. The person who said "I love you" right before they left. Over time, the Skeptic developed what they believe is good discernment. And it is, in some ways. They are often perceptive, clear-eyed, and difficult to deceive. But their discernment has crossed into hypervigilance, and hypervigilance is not the same as wisdom. It is fear wearing the clothes of intelligence.

The cost of the Skeptic pattern is intimacy itself. You cannot be truly close to someone while simultaneously guarding against them. The wall that keeps out the pain also keeps out the love. And the Skeptic, who often privately longs more than most for something solid and real, ends up the loneliest person in the room.

The reframe: your instincts have protected you. But at some point, protection became a prison. Trust doesn't mean being naive. It means being brave enough to let evidence, not fear, make the decision.

SIDEBAR: The Skeptic's greatest challenge is distinguishing between intuition and projection. Not every pattern in a new relationship is a repeat of an old one. Sometimes a person is simply safe, and your nervous system doesn't know the difference yet.

The Four Patterns

a field guide to how we protect ourselves in relationships

---

01 — REACTOR
Emotion leads, action follows

CORE BEHAVIOR
Responds quickly, often intensely, with little space between trigger and reaction.

ROOT FEAR
Loss of control or being powerless — underneath that, a fear of being unseen or invalidated.

PHYSICAL SIGNATURE
Tight chest, shallow breathing, heat in the face or neck, forward-leaning posture, quick gestures.

---

02 — SKEPTIC
Evaluation as self-protection

CORE BEHAVIOR
Questions motives, doubts intentions, analyzes for flaws. Keeps emotional distance by staying in evaluation mode.

ROOT FEAR
Being misled or made vulnerable. At a deeper level, fear of trust leading to betrayal.

PHYSICAL SIGNATURE
Stillness, crossed arms, narrowed eyes, slight head tilt, controlled breathing, minimal expressive movement.

---

03 — RESCUER
Worth earned through being needed

CORE BEHAVIOR
Over-functions for others. Fixes, helps, intervenes — often uninvited. Gains identity through being needed.

ROOT FEAR
Being irrelevant or unworthy unless providing something. Often tied to conditional self-worth.

PHYSICAL SIGNATURE
Leaning in, attentive eye contact, soft tone — paired with tension in shoulders or fatigue in the body.

---

04 — ESCAPIST
Avoidance as a survival strategy

CORE BEHAVIOR
Avoids discomfort through distraction, withdrawal, or numbing. Can look like procrastination or detachment.

ROOT FEAR
Inability to handle emotional intensity or failure. A fear of being overwhelmed or exposed.

PHYSICAL SIGNATURE
Slumped posture, low energy, disengaged eye contact — or restless distraction (phone use, fidgeting).

These patterns are not fixed identities — they are habitual responses that can be observed, named, and changed.

What Your Pattern Feels Like in the Body

Awareness does not live only in the mind. Before you can interrupt a pattern, you need to recognize it in the body because the body moves first. The decision comes after. The pattern has already started.

The **Escapist** feels it as a contraction in the chest and a quiet urge to go somewhere else. Not a dramatic exit. A slow withdrawal. A dimming. The conversation is still happening. You are already partially gone.

The **Rescuer** feels it as a forward lean and a held breath the physical readiness to step in, take on, absorb. Before anyone has asked for anything. Before the situation has fully developed. The body is already in position.

The **Reactor** feels it as heat at the throat and jaw. A tightening. The sensation of something rising before the conscious mind has even processed what triggered it. By the time the words arrive, the body has already decided.

The **Skeptic** feels it as a rapid acceleration of thought the mind running ahead, cataloging evidence, constructing scenarios. It looks like analysis. It is the nervous system building a case for distance before any verdict has been reached.

Notice your body. That is where the pattern tells the truth before your mind gets a chance to rationalize it.

You Probably Recognized Yourself

If you read through those four patterns and felt something, discomfort, recognition, mild irritation, or the specific feeling of being quietly exposed, that's not an accident. These patterns are common because the relational wounds that generate them are common. Most of us didn't grow up with parents who modeled emotionally healthy relationships. Most of us learned love in imperfect, sometimes damaging, sometimes simply incomplete environments. We did the best we could with what we had.

But we're adults now. And continuing to do what we've always done is no longer the best we can do. It's just the most familiar.

A few things worth clarifying before we move forward.

First: most people don't operate exclusively from one pattern. You may see yourself primarily in the Rescuer but recognize real threads of the Skeptic. You may be an Escapist in romantic relationships but a Reactor in family dynamics. Patterns are not rigid boxes. They are tendencies, shaped by context, history, and the specific nervous system of the person across from you.

Second: these patterns are not life sentences. They are starting points. Naming your pattern is not the destination. It is the door. The work that follows this chapter, and what we move into throughout the rest of this book and beyond, is about learning to live on the other side of that door. About building new relational reflexes that serve you instead of sabotage you.

Third: knowing your pattern does not make you exempt from it. I have clients who can describe their Escapist pattern in perfect detail and still go silent for three days when their partner brings up something uncomfortable. Insight is necessary but not sufficient. What transforms insight into change is practice: repeated, intentional, supported practice.

SIDEBAR: Awareness is the beginning. It is not the finish line. Don't confuse knowing the name of your pattern with having broken it.

Naming your pattern is the first act of Phase 1. But it's not the last.

The chapter after this one is about the wound underneath the pattern, the reality of what happens when relational trauma goes unaddressed and what it costs. I want you to read it before we talk about the tool for interrupting the pattern. Because the tool lands differently once you understand what it is actually interrupting. A technique applied to a surface problem produces surface results. What we are going after is deeper than the surface.

The Pattern Beneath the Pattern

Here is the thing that unifies all four of these patterns. The thing that, once you see it, you cannot unsee.

Every single one of them is a response to the same underlying terror: the fear of not being enough to be loved, and the fear of being destroyed by the love you receive.

The Escapist is afraid that closeness will confirm they are fundamentally unworthy of care. The Rescuer is afraid that without their usefulness, they have no relational value. The Reactor is afraid that if they don't fight for visibility, they will be forgotten. The Skeptic is afraid that if they let their guard down, they will be annihilated again.

Different strategies. Same wound.

Which means the path forward is also, at its core, the same for all four:

learning to tolerate the vulnerability of being known, and building the evidence, slowly and deliberately, that being known does not have to mean being abandoned or destroyed.

That is not a weekend project. That is the work. And it is work worth doing. The goal is not to eliminate the pattern. The goal is to stop letting the pattern make decisions for you.

Exercise: The Pattern Activation:
https://go.carloshines.com/book/pattern-activation-log
or Scan the QR Code below

The Wounds We Carry

Most of us have heard of Post Traumatic Stress Disorder, or PTSD, a well-established condition of persistent mental and emotional distress that occurs as a result of injury or severe psychological shock. PTSD symptoms usually involve sleep disturbances and constant, unwelcome revivals of the experience, and it is common in those who have served in combat or who are victims of violent assault, natural disaster, and other potentially life-threatening events.

Post-Traumatic Relationship Syndrome, or **PTRS**, is a newly proposed mental health condition identified as a result of traumatic experiences in intimate relationships. It can be defined as an anxiety disorder that develops after physical, emotional, or psychological abuse experienced in the context of an intimate partner relationship. PTRS evolves from a psychological crisis that exceeds the capacity of the individual's psychic structure to handle it and has debilitating effects on the individual.

Sufferers of PTRS experience similar symptoms to those suffering from PTSD, often experiencing intrusive thoughts, recurring memories, and inappropriate sensory arousal. Oftentimes, sufferers of PTRS experience frequent rumination, vivid flashbacks, nightmares, intense emotional distress, weight loss, shaking, palpitations, sweaty palms, and other anxious symptoms, as well as hypervigilance. Those with PTRS may be unable to sleep or to concentrate fully and may find themselves panicked or angry frequently. Oftentimes, sufferers from PTRS feel they don't deserve a healthy, happy relationship, and find it challenging to trust new romantic partners and, at times, even friends and loved ones. They assume blame for the trauma and isolate themselves from anyone they believe wouldn't understand. Furthermore, they might unconsciously be drawn to unhealthy relationships, and are likely to repeat the past trauma under new circumstances.

However, unlike sufferers of PTSD, who often avoid reminders of the traumatic experience or event, sufferers of PTRS frequently engage in behaviors that perpetuate the trauma, including returning to the abusive partner, entering relationships that trigger the trauma, or engaging in self-destructive behaviors. I see this often in couples who attach to one another through trauma bonds. Those with PTRS don't, or can't, avoid reminders of the trauma, leaving them wholly and continually aware of what happened to them.

Furthermore, in the context of PTSD, the sufferer must witness the traumatic event, whereas in the case of PTRS, sufferers must be directly involved in the trauma. It is essential to note the distinctions that separate PTRS from PTSD. PTRS stems from the fear, mistrust, and traumas that occur exclusively and specifically within relationships.

How Your Pattern Carries the Wound

PTRS does not present the same way in everyone. How it manifests depends significantly on which pattern you are running because your pattern is not separate from your wound. It is the structure the wound built to protect itself.

The Escapist's PTRS tends toward intrusive and arousal symptoms. The body that braces before anything has gone wrong. The hypervigilance that reads closeness as threat even when the threat is nowhere in the room. The withdrawal that happens not because the relationship is dangerous but because the nervous system cannot yet tell the difference between danger and love getting too real.

The Rescuer's PTRS tends toward relational symptoms. The deep, bone-level belief that they are unworthy of love unless they are earning it. The unconscious gravitational pull toward people who need saving. The self-abandonment that feels like generosity until the moment it doesn't, which is usually the moment they realize they have given everything and received very little back.

The Reactor's PTRS tends toward arousal symptoms first and loudest. The body in a near-constant state of fight readiness. The emotional flooding that arrives before the conscious mind has registered danger. The intensity that burns out the emotional safety that sustained intimacy requires.

The Skeptic's PTRS tends toward relational and intrusive symptoms combined. The hypervigilance to betrayal signals the constant scanning, the building of evidence, the interpretation of ordinary behavior as proof of the thing they are most afraid of. The testing behaviors that come from a place of genuine self-protection and do damage anyway.

Your PTRS is not separate from your pattern. It is what your pattern is protecting.

What Does PTRS Look Like in the Individual?

PTRS is not yet recognized as a diagnosable mental health condition in the Diagnostic and Statistical Manual of Mental Disorders, or DSM, but that's not to say it's invalid. Adding a disorder to the DSM usually takes about six to twelve years due to research requirements and proper approvals. Science hasn't yet caught up to culture, and vice versa. At the time of this writing, the American Psychiatric Association isn't able to reach an agreement on all PTRS symptoms or diagnostic criteria. However, they do agree that sufferers from PTRS can experience anxiety, depression, dissociation, personality disorders, and substance abuse. PTRS is a trauma response that occurs during the abuse, which is usually a response of anger, horror, and rage toward the abuser, and after the abuse, the victim may suffer from intrusive, relational, and arousal symptoms.

Over the years, I've worked with plenty of couples who display signs of PTRS. Usually, the symptoms are masked under some other problem in the relationship such as trust, jealousy, or personality clashes. But here's a fact that you won't find in the limited research or online: at the beginning of my practice, only one of the partners in the relationship came to therapy with

PTRS symptoms. But now, both partners are showing up with relationship trauma, lasting trauma that stifles the relationship's health and success. They find themselves in a situation where they are struggling to fix each other while ignoring their own need to heal.

The relationship expectancy is 50/50. I know that sounds harsh, so let me explain. There is no level of compatibility, no amount of love and commitment, no level of consistency or validation, no measurement of trust, and no amount of passion, compassion, or chemistry that can keep together a couple who hasn't properly addressed PTRS on an individual level. As much as we'd like to believe otherwise, you cannot heal yourself while trying to fix your partner.

I travel often for work, and I've heard the airline pre-runway announcements so many times I can repeat them verbatim in my sleep. My daughter was one year old the first time I took her on a plane, and I realized then the gravity of the flight attendant's words: "In the event of a decompression, an oxygen mask will automatically appear in front of you. To start the flow of oxygen, pull the mask towards you. Place it firmly over your nose and mouth, secure the elastic band behind your head, and breathe normally. Although the bag does not inflate, oxygen is flowing to the mask. **If you are traveling with a child or someone who requires assistance, secure your mask on first, and then assist the other person.** Keep your mask on until a uniformed crew member advises you to remove it."

They're telling us, in so few words, to abandon our natural instinct to protect and preserve our children and loved ones, and ignore it, just for a moment. I listened and began wondering, "How is it even remotely possible for me to help her if I'm unconscious, or worse, dead?" The answer is I can't. That's the point. Romantic relationships are much the same. We strongly desire to help, heal, and fix our partners so they can be better, but we ourselves are emotionally unconscious, emotionally numb and lifeless. We must learn to heal ourselves before trying to heal others. More importantly, we must learn to spend time alone while healing because it not only speeds up the process but it also allows for self-evaluation. Address your own trauma, then help those around you. Because if you don't like yourself enough to be alone, why do you think someone else would like being with you?

Simply put, PTRS is, at its core, a trauma response that occurs during the abuse, physically, emotionally, or both, and is usually a response of anger, horror, and rage toward the person who is triggering it. After the abuse, the victim may suffer from intrusive, relational, and arousal symptoms. I want to preface this by saying that in the case of PTRS, something as unsettling as being cheated on can have strong effects that may cause PTRS. I do not want you to think that to experience PTRS, one must have been physically abused. Let's take a look at these symptoms in an effort to better educate ourselves on what they look like and how they may appear.

Intrusive symptoms refer to anything that may cause the sufferer to re-experience or imagine the trauma that occurred. This includes flashbacks and general feelings of absence, intrusive thoughts, fear, anguish, emotional distress, and severe anxiety that causes physical symptoms including shaking, sweating, and odd speech patterns. When reminded of the relationship, sufferers are likely to dissociate, experience immense anxiety, and feel emotional distress. These reminders can be anything from photos, places, names, thoughts, odd objects, or, in many cases, new relationships. Have you said or ever heard someone say, "They did the one thing they promised they wouldn't do"? This is one of many examples of re-experiencing trauma.

Arousal symptoms come from your body's innate fear response. In the case of those suffering from traumatic stress, hyperarousal, or the state of being overstimulated, occurs seemingly spontaneously because the body prepares for abuse. The arousal response causes insomnia, inability to concentrate, irritability, and feelings of anxiety and worry in PTRS sufferers. These symptoms can heavily impede day-to-day functioning. A good example of this would be someone who's been cheated on several times in past relationships and suspects their current partner is cheating on them as well. Suddenly their body goes into arousal mode. Panic, anxiety, elevated heartbeat, and anger ensue.

Relational symptoms are those that relate to the self and interpersonal relationships. Relational symptoms can include feeling as though you don't deserve a happy relationship, being unconsciously drawn to unhealthy relationship dynamics, being untrusting of others, anxiety in new relationships, feelings of blame, sexual dysfunction, and feelings of isolation. Relational symptoms can be just as, if not more, emotionally distressing for sufferers of PTRS. They feel as if they cannot trust others and subsequently blame themselves. We've all heard people say, "I don't trust nobody," or, "I'm waiting for something bad to happen because this relationship is too good to be true," or, "What's wrong with me? Why is it that in every relationship I'm in, I feel so lonely?"

What Causes PTRS?

There are a few key causes of PTRS, the most direct of these being abuse within the context of an intimate relationship. Abuse takes multiple forms. Sufferers may have endured physical abuse, the direct or threatened use of physical, bodily harm, or sexual abuse, including assault, rape, coercion, or misconduct. They may have experienced emotional abuse, including gaslighting, manipulation, and control. Sufferers from PTRS may be experiencing one or all of these. Specifically, PTRS is a human response to the reminders of fear coupled with a strong fear of future abuse. Over time, this fear swells, especially after repeated abuse. As it grows, it leaves doubt, low self-worth, and a lost sense of identity in its wake.

Before we continue, I want to distinguish between toxicity and abuse, because contrary to what you read online, the two terms are not synonymous with one another.

Emotional abuse involves a pattern of behaviors aimed at controlling or manipulating another person's emotions, thoughts, or behavior. Examples of emotional abuse include insults, belittling, gaslighting, withholding affection, and using threats or coercion to gain control over the other person. Emotional abuse can have serious negative impacts on a person's mental health, self-esteem, and overall well-being, and can lead to long-lasting emotional scars.

Toxicity, on the other hand, refers to a broader pattern of negative interactions between two people that may be characterized by frequent arguments, criticism, and negativity. A toxic relationship can involve a lack of empathy, poor communication, and an overall sense of unhappiness or dissatisfaction. While toxicity can be harmful to a relationship and the individuals involved, it may not always involve intentional manipulation or control the way emotional abuse does.

It's important to note that emotional abuse can often be a component of a toxic relationship, and toxicity can sometimes lead to emotional abuse. However, not all toxic relationships involve emotional abuse, and not all emotional abuse occurs within toxic relationships. Understanding the difference matters, because the way you address and heal from each of them is not the same.

The Dangers of Unresolved PTRS

As we previously noted in earlier chapters, we enter relationships to take, not to give. Therefore, it is incredibly common to take the behaviors we learned as a result of abuse, particularly within the context of PTRS, and bring those to our next relationship, which ultimately reinforces our own negative relational beliefs. Many who suffer from PTRS believe they are incapable or unworthy of love, and enter into new relationships with this belief in hand. When they do so, they inherently act out certain negative behaviors that lead to a spiral within the new relationship, often sabotaging it altogether. When the new relationship ends, the sufferer's belief that they cannot be in a happy relationship is reinforced. As with many of the people I've coached, sufferers blame their behaviors on the old relationship, the ex, and do not address their own bleeding. And let me tell you, the bleeding isn't a mere drop of blood. It's an open wound.

We experience traumas that can be processed and healed through therapy, yet it's not unusual for them to go unresolved, often becoming excuses for our own failures and shortcomings. These defective habits, born out of the negative patterns and dysfunctions occasioned by the original traumas, serve to provide us with a convenient rationale to perpetuate our own destructive behaviors. In the context of PTRS, a sufferer might enter another relationship and blame their unhealthy behaviors on their past relationships. Let me reiterate this one fact: it is your responsibility to address your trauma. You cannot take it with you into every new relationship and expect a different result. Our reliance on our own faulty rationale and our unwillingness to confront our pain cost us greatly. We deny our own human agency, squander our potential, and relinquish the very thing that makes us human: our right to choose.

When we use our trauma as a crutch, we handicap our potential to give our full selves to our potential partners. When we enter relationships as fragmented pieces, it exposes us in ways that contribute to our pain rather than healing it.

Some people who are hurting use relationships to escape their pain but quickly realize that an intimate relationship exposes their vulnerabilities. New relationships only allow us to escape the pain temporarily, and when I use the word temporarily, I mean between three and six months. Often, partners will do something, act a certain way, or make a statement that triggers something from our past and may cause us to re-experience a traumatic event.

In the case of PTRS, the partner's behavior, the trigger, isn't usually done on purpose, but to the sufferer, it feels that way. Once the sufferer's vulnerabilities are exposed and if they spiral as they usually do, those vulnerabilities will immediately threaten the relationship. This is why I strongly advise clients to remain single while healing from past trauma and before moving from one relationship to another too quickly. When we move from relationship to relationship without addressing our pain, we endure more pain and inflict it on our new partners, who then leave the relationship carrying pain of their own and engage in similar behaviors. I call it the toxic trauma cycle.

Here is what that cycle looks like in practice. We enter a relationship carrying unhealed wounds. Those wounds get triggered. We wound our partner in response. The relationship ends and both people leave more damaged than when they arrived. Then both people carry that new damage into their next relationship, and the cycle continues. Two people enter, two people leave hurt. Nobody wins. Nobody heals. The only way to break the cycle is to step out of it entirely, do the work alone, and come back to relationships whole enough to build something real.

The past is a vast hiding space with many things kept inside. The present, however, is much different. It is merely a narrow opening we can lean on to re-enact the past's ills if we so choose, or we can decide to start anew. Our relationships can only survive the test of time if we stop holding on to the past. I implore you: stop dragging around your trauma and address it head-on.

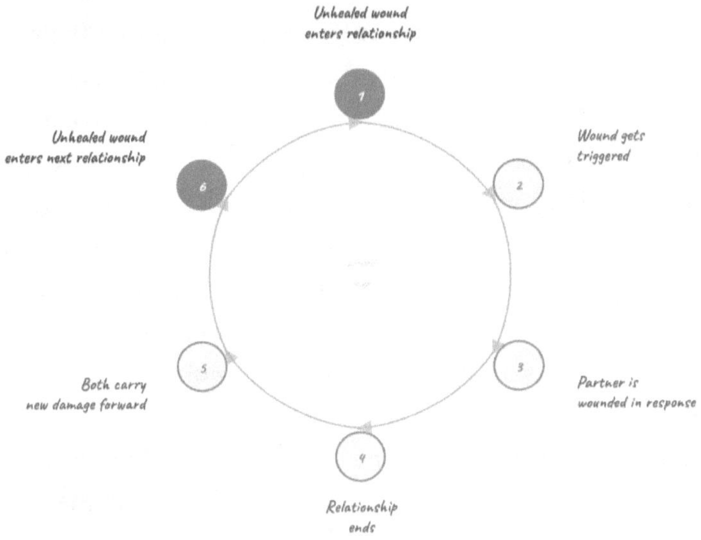

Addressing It Head-On

Because PTRS is not yet a recognized condition in the DSM-5, treatment protocols remain understudied and underdeveloped. However, as more research about the condition comes to light, there are a few methodologies designed by researchers in place to help sufferers reintegrate themselves. That being said, this isn't a diagnostic treatment book. The methods I cover are for your knowledge, and do not take the place of a licensed psychotherapist.

The stages of healing from PTRS are similar to those of other mental health conditions with a few changes. Treatment is separated into four stages: Understanding and Normalization, Acceptance, Integration into the individual's self-concept, and Growth.

Understanding and Normalization refers to the process of helping the sufferer understand the breadth of their trauma and how it impacts their day-to-day life. Sufferers from PTRS are aware that their behavior is abnormal, but may not understand that their symptoms are a normal response to being traumatized. They learn that their states of anxiety and panic are not because they themselves are abnormal, but because the trauma they endured is. They must normalize their feelings to understand that they themselves are not broken. The trauma is what is broken. Therapists can help individuals overcome their generalized fear and replace it with realistic fear. The sufferer is taught regulatory coping skills and learns how to regulate their emotions instead of simply responding to them. Ultimately, they begin to process the trauma.

Reflection and Acceptance are the next steps to healing. Accepting that one is the victim of abuse is not easy, and I highly recommend seeing a licensed therapist who can help with this step. When we process trauma, we find personal meaning in the experience and eventually come to accept that although the experience may not fit our perception of ourselves, we did indeed survive a severely abusive relationship, which required considerable strength. Without acceptance, we cannot move forward and find empowerment.

Integration into the Self-Concept refers to the process of recalibrating one's sense of self after a traumatic event. We must identify the specific beliefs, behaviors, and emotions that have changed after the trauma and learn how these fit into our sense of self. This process asks the person to examine their personality, personal history, and other important relationships. When individuals do this, they gain a strong understanding of what happened and learn how to compartmentalize moving forward. In some cases, a sufferer must come to a rational understanding of the specific reasons they remained in that relationship, such as dependence, low self-esteem, loneliness, anxiety, reliving childhood abuse, or a lack of assertiveness to change or to end the relationship.

Growth refers to the last stage of healing, when the individual gains hope, trust, and control in their own reality. We cannot grow if we are unwilling to change, and it is crucial that sufferers of PTRS gain a sense of self-efficacy, or they will not be able to move forward. A therapist may help a client through assertiveness training and review their progress.

Healing from PTRS does not mean that you are broken. PTRS is a kind of signal. There's a wound present, and it needs renewing. Healing does not require that something needs to be fixed, but rather that it needs to be renewed. Consider how the body heals scars and wounds. Your body's capacity to heal lies in the creation of new cells, not attempting to fix the old ones. Hemostasis occurs to stop bleeding and clear the site of the injury, and a scab forms to protect the area from pathogens. Underneath the scab, cell proliferation begins, and new skin cells are generated and prepared to replace the scab. Angiogenesis further supports wound healing. New blood vessels deliver oxygen and nutrients to the new tissue, promoting its growth and strengthening the skin barrier. Healing from trauma is much like this. We must address the problem, take steps to heal from it, and soon, we will be stronger.

The Reset Ritual™ is the prescription.

This is not a communication technique. Communication techniques fail under activation because by the time you need them, the body has already taken over. The Reset Ritual works before communication begins. It is a nervous system intervention designed to interrupt the pattern at the moment it fires before it makes a decision you will spend weeks recovering from. Here's the three components:

Stated Need. In the moment you feel your pattern activating: the contraction, the heat, the acceleration, the lean you name what you actually need. Not what you want the other person to do. Not what they did wrong. What you need, stated simply and only to yourself. I need to feel seen. I need to feel safe. I need a moment before I respond. The Escapist's challenge here is honesty. The pattern wants to say nothing. Say something, even if only to yourself. The Reactor's challenge is brevity. The body wants volume. One sentence.

Two-Minute Mirror. A brief somatic check-in that interrupts the threat response before it becomes behavior. Sixty seconds of deliberate breathing. Naming what you are feeling in the body without attaching a story to it. Heat at the throat. Tightness in the chest. The urge to leave. This is not meditation. It is a pause. Sixty seconds is enough to give the prefrontal cortex a chance to come back online.

Twenty-Minute Pause. Not avoidance. A structured hold. You do not attempt to resolve the conversation while your nervous system is still in activation. You do not come back to the conversation until twenty minutes have passed and the body has returned to a regulated state. The Escapist will use this pause to actually leave. That is not the tool. The pause is a pause, not an exit. The Skeptic will use it to build a case. That is not the tool either. The twenty minutes are for regulation, not preparation.

You will find the full Reset Ritual with pattern-specific guidance for how each pattern moves through the three steps differently at the link below.

PTRS is a serious condition that requires help from a licensed therapist. If you're suffering from PTRS, there are avenues to help you improve. You're not alone. What happened to you was horrible, but the damage can be addressed. You deserve a chance to move forward. You owe it to yourself. I'm here for you. I'm rooting for you.

Exercise: The Reset Ritual:
https://go.carloshines.com/book/reset-ritual
or Scan the QR Code below

When Ego Runs the Relationship

"I hate shit like this," Sam thought to herself as she stepped out of her Uber. She walked toward the hotel's double doors, accidentally stepping on the hem of her red evening gown not once, but twice. She nodded to the doorman, who motioned over to the elevator across the lobby. Sam pressed the button and watched as the numbers on the glass window increased as the elevator moved toward the top floor. She played with her jacket's lining and thought of Chris, her boyfriend, who said he'd be here by now. Sam checked her phone and didn't see any notifications, none that were important anyway, so she slipped it into her bag. He wasn't usually late. They'd fought the night before about this party. Chris hated Sam's boss, and Sam hated that he kept accusing her of cheating on him. But he'd still promised to come.

The hotel's top-floor event space had been entirely transformed. Servers brought shrimp cocktails, charcuterie, and drinks to guests, and a tower of gourmet cupcakes sat in the corner near a DJ booth. Nearly everyone was there. Three hundred people milled around, commenting on the decor. Sam's company had gone all out for this party, and while Sam liked to be professional and reserved at work, she was gleeful when a server handed her a champagne flute.

Her boss, Jack, meandered over to her. His hair was uncoiffed, his hazel eyes were already bloodshot, and his hands were swollen and red. If she were five or so years younger and single, she'd think he was attractive in a George Clooney kind of way, but Sam was an adult in a committed relationship, and Jack was a walking HR hazard.

"You look," Jack paused, looking her up and down for a few seconds longer than appropriate. "Elegant."

Sam rolled her eyes and laughed a bit. "The invitation said black tie attire."

"That's right," he replied. "But I wasn't really talking about your outfit."

Sam shifted in her heels, wavering just a bit. When is Chris going to get here, she thought, glancing around for a clock.

"Where is your wife?" Sam asked, a little annoyed. Her boss had been on her case since she'd been hired. The other women had warned her about Jack. He took a vested interest in any women employee younger than thirty-five.

"Around, I think." He looked around, and as he did so, she felt Chris's hand graze her arm. She turned to look at Chris, who stood behind her wearing a suit. Sam and Chris had been together for over a year, and she rarely saw him in a suit.

"You're here!" she said, leaning on his shoulder a bit.

"So this is the boyfriend," Jack said with a jovial chuckle. He held out his hand to shake Chris's, but Chris didn't accept the invitation, instead tightening his grip on Sam's waist. Jack recoiled but nodded.

"Yes," Sam told him with a smile. Chris felt rigid next to her, almost shaking.

"Well," Jack began. "It's great to meet you. You couldn't make the barbeque last summer and I had to keep poor Sam company. I was almost hoping you wouldn't come again!" he said with a sarcastic chuckle. Sam felt Chris's hand tighten even more.

"I'm here," Chris said. "No need." His eyes were darkened and his hand, still tight around her waist, felt hot to the touch.

"Well, we love your little lady around here," Jack said. "She's our star performer."

Chris nodded and Jack walked away, sensing the tension between Sam and her boyfriend.

The rest of the party was a bit of a blur, partly because of the champagne. Sam joked with co-workers and sipped her drink while Chris stood stoically in the corner.

A few hours later, the two got on the elevator. Sam hoped someone would join them, but found herself alone with Chris.

"What the hell was that?" he bellowed. He banged his fist against the glass door.

"What was what?" she asked, though she knew the answer.

"Your boss," Chris began. "You're sleeping with your boss?"

"That's crazy, Chris," muttered Sam. Her body was frozen in its place.

"He all but came on to you right there in front of me!" Chris yelled. "Don't be stupid, Sam."

"I'm not being stupid and he didn't come on to me in front of you," she replied, a little louder this time.

"He made a fool out of me." Chris paced around the elevator. "He made me look like an idiot. You know why I couldn't go to that stupid barbeque and you didn't even say anything?"

"I didn't want to air out your dirty laundry!" Sam yelled back. "You always do this."

"No," Chris yelled. "You always do this. You parade yourself around and flirt to get ahead. That's what this is."

"I don't flirt to get ahead, Chris," Sam pursed her lips. "You're being childish. This is nothing."

"It's not nothing!" he screamed, slamming his hand against the elevator wall. Sam prayed the ride would end. She played with her dress's fringe. Her hands shook. "I'm just worried about you," he said.

The elevator dinged, and the two walked out to their Uber.

What you just watched was a Reactor pattern in full ego activation.

Chris did not decide to escalate. His pattern escalated. The perceived threat to his sense of self, his ego's grip on the relationship, his identity as Sam's protector triggered a physical and emotional response that bypassed logic entirely. By the time they were in the elevator, the nervous system had already taken over. The ego was simply the vehicle it drove.

Every pattern uses ego differently. The Reactor's ego defends through escalation and visibility. If I am loud enough, I cannot be ignored. The Rescuer's ego defends through indispensability. If I am useful enough, I cannot be abandoned. The Skeptic's ego defends through intellectual armor, a cold, constructed distance that passes itself off as discernment. The

Escapist's ego simply disappears. Gone before anyone can make demands on it.

The ego does not run your relationship on its own. It runs it through your pattern. And your pattern has a very specific playbook.

Ego is a term commonly associated with processes or reactions in which the individual is the center of attention. **Egoism** refers to a motivation to act in one's own self-interest, a behavior that is quite natural and ubiquitous. An individual is said to be egoistic when their actions are focused solely on fulfilling their own wants and needs, which is a common occurrence in human behavior. Simply put, the English word ego is the Latin word for I. If you were writing "I love you" in Latin, you'd write ego amo te. Ego, then, is the conscious, decision-making part of you that you regard as I. When you say, "I dislike that person," or "I've decided to change jobs," or "I dream of becoming a millionaire," the I you use is your ego.

The issue is this: the ego doesn't have any skills that lend well to relationship formation. The ego is committed to always putting itself first and is too wrapped up in itself to care about others. Therefore, the ego often uses manipulation as a means to both give and receive love and, to protect ourselves, the ego resorts to resistance, arguing, fighting, sarcasm, put-downs, depression, withdrawal, aggression, frustration, passive-aggressiveness, revenge, disrespectful gestures, intolerance, blame, competition, distrust, resentment, and self-doubt. When filtered through our ego, the act of expressing love metamorphoses into an urge for authority and domination over the other person. In the example, Chris needed to control Sam and resorted to aggressive behaviors when he felt his control being threatened, banging his fist against the elevator wall, and then put her down with his accusations. This need for control, which stems from the ego, is a major hindrance to fostering true love. The ego's choices become the very obstacles to love and our relationships.

Egotistical love refers to a kind of love where an individual is more concerned about what they gain from a relationship than the actual person they're with. This kind of love is not selfless. It is based on specific conditions and what can be possessed.

True love involves giving without expecting anything in return. The individual loves the other person for who they are as opposed to what they can offer. Ego love is not love, and you must be able to differentiate between the two to establish healthy and meaningful relationships. Ego love comes with strings attached. The individual says they love the other person but then expects them to make personal changes. And if the other person fails to make these changes, the love fades away. It is conditional and wrought with expectations. The egoist prioritizes their own happiness. There is a hidden agenda within ego love, and therefore it is not genuine. It lacks love's fundamental qualities of selflessness and unconditional affection. It is taking, but not giving. The egoist loves the other person not for who they are, but for what they can provide, making the love ultimately transactional. Ego love is the antithesis of unconditional love.

Understanding the Roots of Ego

To effectively manage our ego and its impact on our relationships, we must understand its roots and development. Our ego forms during childhood and is influenced by a variety of factors including our early experiences, our relationships with our caregivers, our attachment patterns, social and cultural contexts, and gender. When we examine these, we gain insight into the sources of our ego and can work toward cultivating a balanced and compassionate sense of self. Understanding the roots of the ego is a critical component of developing healthy relationships.

The relationship between a child and their caregiver is among the key influences on the development of our ego. When a child receives consistent and responsive care from a caregiver, they develop a sense of security and trust in the world around them. Their secure attachment lays the foundation for healthy self-esteem and a balanced sense of self. However, when children receive inconsistent or neglectful care from their caregivers, they are susceptible to developing insecure attachment patterns that lead to personal feelings of inadequacy, mistrust, and a desire for control over the world around them. Our experiences with both praise and criticism impact our developing ego. When we receive positive, consistent feedback for our accomplishments, we develop a strong sense of confidence and self-worth. However, when we are frequently criticized or judged, or when we experience inconsistent praise, we may develop a sense of inadequacy or a need to prove ourselves to those around us.

Social and cultural context plays an additional role in the ego's development. In cultures that value individualism and competition, such as Western culture, individuals may experience increased pressure to develop both a strong sense of self and to assert their dominance over others. In contrast, in cultures that value collectivism and cooperation and emphasize the importance of relationships and interconnectedness as opposed to individual achievement, such as many Eastern cultures, the individual might develop a more collective, empathetic, and less assertive ego.

As we previously noted in earlier chapters, these socialization experiences seek to confine people in their roles. However, in modern society, these roles do not hold true across the board. With enough self-awareness and intention, we can work to manage our ego and develop healthier patterns of relating to ourselves and others.

How Your Pattern Uses Ego

The roots of the ego are universal. What the ego defends, and how, is pattern-specific.

The Reactor's ego defends through escalation. When the fear of being unseen is activated, the ego converts it into volume. Into accusation. Into the kind of intensity that demands acknowledgment even at the cost of the relationship it is trying to protect. The behavior says: respond to me. The wound underneath it says: I am terrified you will forget I am here.

The Rescuer's ego defends through martyrdom. The giving is real. The resentment building underneath it is equally real. The ego keeps score in a ledger the Rescuer denies keeping. When the ledger fills up, it does not present itself as anger. It presents itself as exhaustion, withdrawal, or a quiet devastation that neither person has language for. The behavior says: look how much I give. The wound says: please love me without conditions.

The Skeptic's ego defends through superiority. The armor is intelligence, discernment, the apparent wisdom of someone who has seen enough to know better. It holds people at a measured distance and calls the distance good judgment. The behavior says: I am not fooled. The wound says: I am terrified of being fooled again.

The Escapist's ego defends through absence. It does not need to be the loudest in the room. It simply leaves the room. Quietly, often without announcement, in ways that can look like independence and feel, to the person left behind, like disappearance. The behavior says: I don't need this. The wound says: I need this so much that wanting it has become unbearable.

The Destructive Role of Ego in Romantic Relationships

While having a healthy ego is necessary for a fulfilling life, it can also be a key source of conflict within relationships. The ego is often the driving force behind our behaviors and actions in both positive and negative ways. When our ego is healthy, we feel confident, secure, and assertive. We are more likely to express ourselves honestly and remain open to feedback and criticism. However, when our ego becomes inflated or overly dominant, we might experience feelings of superiority, arrogance, and entitlement. It is this part of the ego that makes it difficult to form and maintain healthy relationships with others.

Possession and control are among the primary ways ego can destroy romantic relationships. We seek to control and possess our partners as though they are video game characters, not real people. One of my greatest pet peeves is hearing people say "this is my husband" or "she's my girlfriend" as if we own, have possession over, or control our partners' agency. It is this same attitude that causes couples who date for ten years before getting married to break up and divorce within the first three years of marriage. We allow the word marriage to flip a switch in our ego that designates our husband, wife, mate, or life partner as our sole possession. We then start to function and act as though we have full authority to control what they do and how and when they do it. A marriage license is not the same as a dog license. Your partner is not your property.

Defensiveness is another destructive behavior that results from an overinflated ego. When our ego is unduly attached to our desires or opinions, we risk becoming defensive, dismissive, or aggressive toward our partners, especially when they challenge us, interact with others we perceive as a threat to the relationship, or offer us feedback.

Ego, Anger, and Jealousy in Romantic Relationships

Anger and jealousy are both incredibly powerful emotions, and within the context of romantic relationships, they are almost always ego-driven. Understanding how they work together is more useful than treating them as separate problems, because at their core, they come from the same place.

When we're angry, really fuming, we struggle to express ourselves calmly and with clarity, ultimately leading to damaged feelings that create a cycle of escalating conflict. Think back to the story at the beginning of the chapter. When Chris was angry with Sam, he said many hurtful things he can no longer take back. What he said damaged the relationship's trust, possibly irreparably.

Anger also impacts our ability to empathize with others. When we are angry, our focus shifts entirely inward. We only see our own thoughts and feelings. As a result, we struggle to put ourselves in the perspective of our partners, causing a sense of isolation and disconnection that breeds a lack of emotional intimacy and mutual understanding. Anger is useful in physical fights but it is the antithesis of logic. It's a trick of the mind meant to push you into fight or flight mode. And you cannot think clearly when you're in fight or flight. No one does. Remove your anger and you will find clarity.

Jealousy operates through the same mechanism. When our ego becomes bruised or threatened, it often produces jealousy as its defense. Jealousy tends to generate feelings of accusation and blame, leaving the other partner feeling misunderstood and unheard. Chris struggled greatly with jealousy. A seemingly small, joking comment from Sam's boss was enough for Chris to become enraged. He perceived Sam's boss as a threat to his sense of self and his grip on the relationship. When his ego became aroused, he flew into a blind rage, blaming Sam, who was at no fault, for her boss's actions. Sam is left feeling confused, hurt, and undermined. She didn't ask for Jack's attention and made efforts to redirect his focus.

When our ego is overly attached to our sense of self-worth, we feel threatened by our partner's interactions with others we perceive as more successful, attractive, or desirable. In the case of Chris and Sam, Chris's ego, his sense of self-worth, was inflated, and when he felt his sense of self threatened, he flew into a rage, degrading his partner and acting irrationally. The ego breeds anger, and anger breeds jealousy, and both have the capricious capacity to shatter a relationship's foundation.

Furthermore, jealousy has a profound impact on an individual's emotional well-being. The intense negative emotions associated with it often cause feelings of anxiety, depression, and low self-esteem that affect an individual's happiness. If left unchecked, these emotions can eventually infect friendships and work life as well. Jealousy causes a cycle of negative interactions between partners that only serves to exacerbate damage already done to the relationship.

To overcome ego, anger, and jealousy's negative impact on our romantic relationships, we must develop self-awareness and strong emotional regulation skills, cultivate empathy and compassion for our partners, and improve our communication strategies. Working with a counselor or therapist to identify patterns that lead to your anger will be of great benefit, not only for the health of your relationships but most importantly, for yourself. Couples who participate in relationship intervention programs that focus on developing emotional regulation skills and improving communication show significant improvements in relationship satisfaction and reductions in conflict and aggression. Why?

Because the ego does not create conflict from scratch. It runs through a feedback loop that was already in motion one that began long before the argument started and will continue long after it ends, unless you learn to recognize it.

I call it the gridlock loop. And every pattern has one.

The Reactor and Escapist most commonly run what I call the pursue-withdraw loop. One person escalates to get a response. The other withdraws to get relief. The escalation increases the withdrawal. The withdrawal increases the escalation. Neither person is doing something wrong. Both patterns are doing exactly what they were built to do. And the loop runs.

The Rescuer and Skeptic most commonly run the over-function/under-function loop. One person absorbs more and more responsibility, emotional, logistical, relational, while the other, often without realizing it, recedes. The over-functioner eventually collapses or erupts. The under-functioner is surprised every time.

The Gridlock Decoder is a tool for identifying which loop is most active in your relationship and what the loop is actually protecting. When you can name the loop, you can interrupt it. When you cannot name it, it runs indefinitely, and you keep having the same argument in different rooms, in different years, with the same result.

Most of us forget that our partner's experiences are not your own, and that's okay. As we discussed earlier in this book, similarities bond but differences build. The goal is not to eliminate disagreement from your relationship. The goal is to stop letting your ego run the disagreement for you.

Exercise: The Gridlock Decoder: https://go.carloshines.com/book/gridlock-decoder

or Scan the QR Code below

Removing the Mask

Ashley and Jose met online, just as thousands of couples do in the digital age. Ashley believed she was swiping right on a well-renowned college professor. Jose, the smiling, jovial, established man had been published in multiple large publications, ran his own research lab, and taught graduate courses at a prestigious university in California. Jose too swiped on an established young woman. Ashley was a svelte, successful real estate agent and lover of fitness. Here is a timeline of events in their whirlwind relationship.

Months 1 through 4

Their first few dates were magical. They dined at some of their town's most established restaurants, walked along the beach before sunset, and went on a trip to the mountains together. Jose was everything Ashley had hoped for: handsome, young, established in his field, and a master at chivalry. Ashley was Jose's dream girl. He'd longed for someone passionate, driven, classy, and dedicated.

Their first fight was much like the fights you see in movies. Ashley had been out one night with friends and, before she left her apartment, snapped a quick photo of her outfit, which consisted of a small, black crop top and a pair of leather shorts that revealed the bottom half of her butt cheeks. She'd posted it to Instagram for her followers to see, and for the rest of the night, her phone lit up sporadically with like notifications.

While she was out that night, Jose called her, but she didn't notice. She and her friends sipped their drinks, dancing the night away, while he called her repeatedly, leaving angry messages. She didn't check her phone until she was in her Uber on the way home, and she called him back.

"What is this bullshit?" Jose screamed into the phone, clearly irate.

"What is what?" she asked innocuously, feigning naivety.

"The photos," he said, still yelling. "You're naked. It's all over your feed."

"I'm not naked," she replied, trembling. "I have clothes on."

"You're a whore, that's what you are," he continued. Ashley could hear his voice reverberating into the phone. "You're fake, just like everyone else."

He hung up, and Ashley began to cry in the back of the Uber, unaware of what to do. For as long as she could remember, Ashley suffered from low self-esteem, being bullied by schoolmates and family members for her weight. As she grew into her body, the negative attention she received became more positive. Instead of jeers, her male classmates would smile, or even stare when she walked by. She liked the attention and figured she'd use it to her advantage. When the internet boomed, she decided to capitalize on it. She could use social media to garner the validation she had so craved as a child.

Months 5 through 10

One Friday, Ashley and Jose went to a five-star restaurant overlooking the water, dining on calamari, steaks, and lobster mac and cheese. Both of them posted their meals on social media, garnering more likes and profile views. Ashley and Jose stayed on their phones throughout the meal, responding to their comments, spending little time talking to one another.

When it came time to pay the bill, Jose pulled out his credit card, handing it to the waiter without a glance. After a few short minutes, the waiter returned, handing Jose's card back to him.

"Sir," the waiter said sheepishly. "It wouldn't go through."

"It wouldn't go through?" Jose put his phone down and raised his voice. "What do you mean it didn't go through? I barely have a credit limit." He looked to Ashley for confirmation, and she nodded at the waiter with raised eyebrows.

"It didn't go through. It said you'd reached your maximum. Do you have another method of payment?" asked the waiter.

Jose reached into his pocket, pulling out his wallet. He went through his cards, pulling them out one by one. "Here," he said, almost throwing the card at the waiter. "This will work."

Ashley grew nervous, tapping her foot against the hardwood flooring. When the waiter returned, he handed the card back to Jose, shaking his head, signaling that this card didn't work either. Ashley handed the waiter her own credit card, hoping it too would work.

"What was that?" she asked when they finally left for their car.

"He was an idiot," Jose said, puffing out his chest in a way Ashley found disgusting.

"Do you have enough money?" Ashley replied. "We don't have to go out all the time. I can…"

"You can what?" Jose cut in. "I have plenty of money. Shut it." His ego had been bruised, and he stormed to the car without another word.

Later that night, Ashley did a little internet digging. She found that Jose didn't teach at the university and was instead a high school biology teacher. Not only that, but he'd declared bankruptcy not once, but twice. She was appalled, but kept the information to herself. She too had secrets, and she didn't want to anger Jose.

It came time for Jose to meet Ashley's family, and he was excited to do so. She said her dad was a successful real estate mogul and the head of the household. Ashley told him she'd grown up in a wealthy area just outside of Los Angeles. They'd had a house staff and everything. But when it came time for Jose to meet her dad, he was shocked when he pulled up to a dilapidated, two-bedroom rambler in a seedy part of town.

The visit went fine, but during the drive home, Jose said little, ignoring Ashley's attempts at conversation. When he dropped her off, she said, "Thanks for coming," before trying to open her car door.

"You're a liar," said Jose, looking down at his lap.

"I didn't mean to lie. I just…"

"But you did lie." He finally looked at her. Jose spoke softly, like he was about to burst. Ashley was terrified he would.

"I didn't mean to," she replied, settling back in her seat, hoping they could talk about it.

"You're a goddamn liar," Jose screamed, slamming his flattened hand against the steering wheel.

"I don't need this," Ashley replied, opening up the door to leave. As she did, Jose grabbed her arm, pulling her back into the car. "Stop!" she yelled, trying to free herself. "All you do is lie!" he kept yelling, his face red.

"Really Jose, I'm the liar?" she paused for a moment. "Are you sure you want to have this conversation with me? Because I know you don't work at the university!" she snapped, pulling her arm free. "You lied too. You didn't have the guts to admit it, so don't sit there lecturing me!"

Jose paused, leaning back in his seat. She was right. He didn't work at the university. Both Ashley and Jose had secrets. Jose was in credit card debt for the third time, and as their relationship progressed, they began showing their true colors. He wasn't a gentleman, but an angry, manipulative fraud. And Ashley wasn't an ideal loving girlfriend, but a self-preserving woman who lied about her background in order to come across as more established and polished. She revealed that yes, she'd grown up impoverished, often in foster care, and she'd worked hard so she'd never have to live like that again. But in the process, she had lied and manipulated him as well. Her real estate business was failing. She made it appear as though she had over a dozen employees and fifty agents working for her, but Jose quickly found out that her business was a sole proprietorship. It was her and her alone. She too was in debt, just like Jose.

Months 11 through 14

After that night, the two didn't speak of what they'd learned of one another. They retreated to social media, starting a couple's page on TikTok where they posted their forays through Beverly Hills. They kept up their appearances online, appearances that were much different than the reality they truly lived. They amassed a large following and began making money on social media. Ashley and Jose spent every penny.

Around month eleven, cracks began to form. Both Ashley and Jose felt they couldn't trust each other. Their relationship was crumbling as it was built on lies. They fought often but rarely admitted what their fights were truly about: the lies they'd spent so long cultivating. When they fought, Jose lashed out, yelling and even ripping up the photos on Ashley's corkboard. Ashley grew depressed, curated more lies, and increased her time spent on social media.

When Ashley and Jose contacted me, they told me they needed a little help resolving some of their issues. Ashley told me they'd been together for just about a year and wanted tips on how to maintain and strengthen their bond. She spoke softly on the phone, her voice sounding like that of a Disney Princess. Jose, on the other hand, was adamant that nothing was wrong. They were happy. Just look at their profiles online! I discerned the subterfuge they'd attempted to orchestrate when I flew out to California to meet them.

I wasn't the least bit surprised when Ashley told me their relationship began to unravel around month five. Most people can fake facets of who they are: characteristically, morally, spiritually, emotionally, financially, and externally in terms of career development. But this charade can only last for about four to six months before people reveal their true selves.

They remained adamant in our sessions, keeping up their masks, but the Ashley and Jose I came to know weren't the same couple that dined at Nobu every Saturday and enjoyed vacations on white sand beaches. Ashley was deeply insecure and in a state of denial about her life and the relationship. Jose was shallow, self-centered, and had a hair-trigger temper. I came to realize the breadth of their lies, deceit, and the masks they put on in layers. A relationship built on lies was doomed for failure. They were together for a year and a half, and their relationship ended in a messy, awful breakup. Between you and me, I'm surprised it lasted that long.

What Ashley and Jose built was a relationship between two masks. Not two people.

Jose's mask was the established academic authoritative, chivalrous, financially secure. Underneath it was a Reactor pattern running on ego: the hair-trigger temper, the controlling behavior when his sense of self felt threatened, the aggression that arrived when the performance became unsustainable.

Ashley's mask was the generationally wealthy professional, polished, successful, desirable. Underneath it was a pattern built on years of seeking validation from external sources because internal sources had never been reliable. Her social media following was not vanity. It was a nervous system finding the consistent positive response it had never received in the rooms that mattered most.

The mask does not create the pattern. It hides it.

The Reality of Masking

The modern dating landscape is more accessible and simultaneously more complex than ever before. Much of the modern dating experience is characterized by the first impression. As you swipe away on Tinder, Hinge, or Bumble, you're forced to make a quick, instinctual decision. The other people on whom you're swiping left or right have taken steps to curate a specific first impression, and that is solely the impression on which you act. However, this impression is curated with a specific goal in mind, to find a potential partner, and to achieve this goal, individuals highlight their positive attributes and capitalize on their greater perceived control over their own self-presentation.

This curation process is a form of masking. And as we navigate the intricate web of relationships we were never formally taught how to have, we employ masking techniques to present ourselves in the most favorable light. However, masking can have serious negative consequences, particularly within the context of dating. We all seek to put our best foot forward, but we run the risk of taking it too far.

Here is where the pattern comes in.

The mask you wear in early dating is not random. It is your pattern's most socially acceptable face, the version of yourself that keeps the wound protected while appearing available enough to attract what you are looking for.

The Escapist masks as low maintenance. Easy to be around, uncomplicated, pleasantly undemanding. The mask works until the other person wants more depth, more presence, more permanence and realizes the ease was not ease at all. It was managed distance.

The Rescuer masks as selfless. Generous, attentive, the person who always shows up. The mask works until the resentment that was never voiced accumulates into something that can no longer be contained by more giving.

The Reactor masks as passionate. Intense, romantic, fully committed from the beginning. The mask works until the passion turns and the intensity that felt like love starts feeling like threat.

The Skeptic masks as discerning. Thoughtful, measured, someone who does not give themselves away easily. The mask works until the testing starts and the other person realizes the warmth they were promised is not coming.

Your mask is not a lie you tell consciously. It is your pattern's opening position. And like all opening positions, it eventually has to give way to what is actually there.

Impression management, or masking as I prefer to call it, refers to the conscious and subconscious processes by which individuals attempt to influence others' perceptions of them. Impression management involves creating a new, desired image or maintaining a current image, and it results from the individual caring a great deal about how they appear to those around them. We engage in it to achieve a certain result, and it has important implications in social settings. Most, if not all, of life's important events and happenings are contingent on our ability to make favorable impressions during social interactions. Carefully curating your online presence, emphasizing your own positive qualities, and downplaying those qualities you find to be negative are all examples of masking.

Because we engage in masking to achieve what we perceive to be desirable results, the habit is often recreated in the context of dating, particularly during the early stages. When we date and form opinions about potential romantic partners, we adapt our behaviors to convey information to one another. We want to ensure a positive first impression of ourselves, so we inherently cultivate a version of ourselves that we feel the other person will find valuable or interesting. Think back to our example. Jose and Ashley both cultivated images of themselves to attract one another. Ashley created an image of a successful, generationally wealthy real estate agent, and Jose tried to embody the image of an established, chivalrous academic.

What happens next is where it gets interesting.

Authenticity Erosion is the first consequence of sustained masking, and it may be the most damaging. When individuals consistently try to project an idealized version of themselves, they eventually lose touch with who they really are. Over time, as individuals attach themselves to a specific picture of who they'd like to be, they come to believe that image is really them, when in reality, the image is simply a mirage. They lose their sense of self, leaving them feeling lost, confused, and in some cases, depressed. If you don't know who you are, you can't expect another person to know or accept you either. Authenticity erosion was one crack in Ashley and Jose's foundation. It prevented them from developing the deep, emotional connection that is crucial for a long-lasting, fulfilling relationship and ultimately led to the end of theirs.

Impression management is also a self-perpetuating cycle. The more time an individual invests in it, the more they fear being exposed as imperfect. When that fear becomes overwhelming, they invest even more time masking, adding additional layers of lies and deception. What they're ultimately afraid of is not rejection of who they masked themselves to be. It's rejection of who they really are.

Misrepresentation of reality is another consequence, and it refers to the phenomenon where individuals do not present themselves in a truthful way. A person might exaggerate their personal interests or accomplishments to present a more curated, polished version of themselves that is far from realistic, exactly as Jose and Ashley did. In the context of romantic relationships, misrepresentation of reality creates a power imbalance. One partner, the one who isn't doing the misrepresenting, may feel deceived and manipulated, while the other enjoys living behind their mask. As a result, both partners feel resentment and distrust toward one another, leading to the breakdown of their relationship. In romantic relationships, almost always, both partners wear masks. But more likely than not, one of them maintains this facade longer than the other and in far greater falsehood.

Dependence on external validation is the third consequence, and it shows up in both Ashley and Madison from the previous chapter. When we focus so heavily on creating a specific impression, we become reliant on how others respond to that impression rather than on our own sense of self. Over time, dependence on external validation leads to a diminished sense of control and the perpetuation of even more impression management behaviors. We keep needing the likes, the compliments, the validation, because without them we feel as though the mask might slip.

Here is the paradox that ties all three of these consequences together. Impression management is supposed to give us control over how we're perceived. But in practice, individuals who engage in it inadvertently relinquish a certain degree of control over their dating experience, leading to decreased agency and lower satisfaction in their relationships. Studies reveal that impression management and this loss of agency have detrimental effects on our emotional well-being. The behavior that was meant to be proactive actually contributes to feelings of loneliness. One potential explanation is that impression management leads to inauthenticity and incongruence between an individual's presented self and their true self. This leads to difficulty forming genuine connections with others, and in the context of romantic relationships, to feelings of uncertainty and insecurity.

When we take masking a few steps too far, we relinquish the very control we were trying to establish. My father would call it a catch twenty-two. On one hand, impression management fuels our ego and gives us a sense of control. On the other, we relinquish the control we so desire, leading to relational dysfunction.

In the context of dating and romantic relationships, masking becomes a serious issue around the four to six-month mark, as seen in our example at the beginning of the chapter. As Ashley and Jose grew closer and their lives became more intertwined, they could no longer maintain the effort necessary to continue their facade. After about six months of dating, couples can no longer keep up with the image they procured. It requires more effort and energy than they have available, and this is when the true self becomes visible. This leads to cracks, and in the case of Ashley and Jose, a complete breakdown in trust.

Impression management is a perfectly normal, human behavior that lends well to certain social situations, particularly those that depend on a positive first impression. However, when masking behaviors go too far or are used as a crutch or manipulation tactic, individuals suffer from a lost or obscured sense of self and may be unable to form meaningful relationships with others.

The goal is not to walk into every first date with your most embarrassing stories and darkest secrets on the table. The goal is to close the gap, over time, between who you present yourself to be and who you actually are. Because the relationship you build on that gap will collapse the moment the gap is discovered. And the gap is always discovered.

Congrats! You have just completed Phase 1.

Remove the Gridlock. Four chapters. The pattern named. The wound traced. The ego examined. The mask identified. None of that was light work. None of it was meant to be.

Here is what Phase 1 accomplished: it gave you a language for what has been happening underneath your relationships. Not the surface arguments. Not the incompatibility explanations. The actual operating system. The pattern, the wound, the ego, the mask, all of it named. All of it visible in a way it was not when you opened this book.

Recalibration cannot happen while gridlock is still in place. You have removed it. What comes next is not more assessment. It is reconstruction. The next section is Phase 2 of the Re/Model Framework™: Recalibrate the Connection. Its job is to rebuild what the pattern has damaged. Not to go back to what you had. To build forward toward something neither of you has had yet.

The ground has been cleared. Now lets go and build.

III

Recalibrate

Phase 2 begins here.
Remove the Gridlock is behind you. You have named the pattern.
You understand where it came from and what it has cost you.
That is not small work. Most people spend years in therapy
arriving at exactly that clarity, if they arrive at it at all. You have
it now.

Before You Fall in Love

What Recalibrate the Connection asks of you is different. Not more excavation. Not more looking backward at the wound. Forward. Toward the foundation that has to exist before love can hold.

And that foundation does not begin with romance. It begins with friendship.

Ross and David were polar opposites in every sense of the term. Ross, a straight-laced man from Connecticut who worked in finance, was a self-proclaimed numbers guy. His whole life, he'd been drawn to numbers and logic, and if he got a little too drunk at dinner, would often regale his time as a high school mathlete. David would chuckle each time he did so, calling Ross his nerd. David, on the other hand, worked in art curation. David had grown up in Brooklyn and often admired the Manhattan landscape. As he and Ross walked home from dinner, he pointed out the differences in architecture between buildings, commenting on their historical origin. David and Ross were a bit of a black cat and golden retriever couple. David was loud, sarcastic, and colorful, and Ross had a melancholy that often kept to himself. The only colors in his wardrobe were navy and light blue, and at every available opportunity, David would comment on his poor color coordination skills.

As he lay awake one night, Ross scrolled through his phone. Next to him, David snored loudly, and their shared corgi curled up between them. His boss had sent him an email, even though it was nearly midnight, and Ross was quick to reply. But as he did so, he noticed another notification pop up from Instagram. Bored and not the least bit sleepy, he clicked on the pop-up, which led him to a friend's recent post. The post itself wasn't anything special, just his friend and some others at a park near the river, but in the background, he noticed his ex-boyfriend, holding a coffee cup, smiling.

Suddenly, in the way memories often do, Ross recalled his last relationship. The breakup had been anything but amicable, ending in both of them eventually blocking the other. The sex had been great. They'd met at a bar in Hell's Kitchen, and that night, Ross took the ex back to his place, and things progressed from there. They'd dated for about six months, and most of their dates, he hesitated to call them that, were of the bar and hookup variety. In fact, now that Ross was thinking about it, he couldn't recall much else about the ex, save for his favorite drink, a dry martini.

So what was different about David then? Ross thought to himself. He clicked on the ex's profile and began scrolling through his recent photos. Each was taken out at various bars around Lower Manhattan. The ex wasn't ugly by any means, and Ross recalled loving how committed he'd been to the gym, but he couldn't shake the images of them fighting over FaceTime the night they'd ended. The ex had cheated.

Ross and David met through mutual friends. After his breakup, Ross's co-worker thought he could use an afternoon out, and they'd gone to meet up with some other friends at a coffee shop just north of the area where they worked. David had been among the friends. Ross remembered chatting with David about his coffee order, a black Americano, and the two bonded over their mutual disdain of the West Village, claiming the area was much too gentrified, too young. Over time, Ross and David became friends, going out to coffee, lunch, and later, dinner. They had inside jokes. Once, David burned his mouth on a very hot plate of French toast at brunch. They laughed with one another and developed an amicable friendship.

Ross remembered the night he'd asked David out. He'd been to a work dinner with his co-worker, the one who'd introduced them. She'd asked how things were going, and all Ross could talk about was the movie he'd seen with David the weekend previous. She'd suggested he ask him out, and that's just what he'd done. Ross, over text message, asked David on a date, a real one, and said he'd pay. David loved the text, and soon enough, they made their relationship official. The last ten months were a blur. David and Ross moved into a one-bedroom, rescued their corgi, and went on their first vacation together.

But at that moment, Ross couldn't quite recall what was different about his relationship with David. Something was. He knew that much. He trusted David implicitly and loved him for who he was. David wasn't perfect, and Ross knew that. Ross wasn't perfect either. Their relationship too was far from perfect. They fought about Ross's work hours and David's spending, but overall, the two were happy.

Then Ross had a bit of a personal epiphany. He and David were friends first, and lovers second. Their sex life was, in Ross's eyes, in need of improvement, but their relationship was more than just drunken sex. It was first about the friendship, and second about the love the two held for each other. And over time, Ross had come to appreciate this.

He turned off his phone and, for a while, listened to David and the dog's snores materialize over the street noise outside. After an hour or so, he fell asleep to the sounds coming from his partner, whom he'd grown to truly, irrevocably love.

The Friends-First Framework

How do you make friends? Is there a process or script you follow? Where do you meet potential friends? Most adults meet friends in the workplace, community areas or restaurants, college, or, more recently, online. The process of friendship formation varies greatly. Personally, I prefer to ask people to have coffee first. Over time, the potential friend and I meet at restaurants and movie theatres, then spend time at their place, and perhaps then at mine. Finally, at some point, we would meet each other's families, including our pets. Communication, at first, consists of surface-level questions and polite text messages before becoming deeper, more personal, and building off the information I've come to know about the other person.

I'm extremely observant and cautious when making friends. I don't let many people get close to me, so when I do, I must see something special in them. Making friends has, at times, been a difficult task for me, not because I don't want friends or because I don't like people, but because people have grossly disappointed me in the past. And I, like many others, believed that when I trust someone, they will fail me. As a result, when meeting new people, I keep up a defensive guard. Some people believe that you should trust others until they prove to you otherwise, but I believe the reverse. I do not give others the benefit of the doubt. I have zero trust in others by default, so they have to earn it with me over time. In relationships, both romantic and platonic, I have been crossed many times, so for a long time, it was difficult to realize that not everyone was going to eventually hurt me.

It wasn't until a decade ago that I came to realize that the more time I spent with potential friends, the more our conversations became deeper and more seminal. And the deeper these conversations became, the more our friendship flourished. There is something inherently special about building friendships with both different and like-minded people. After all, if everyone in your circle thinks like you, you're in a rather close-minded circle.

What is more exceptionally powerful, however, is when a friendship turns into a romance. I'm about to make a case for that, but first, I'd like you to remove all of your emotional walls and barriers to entry. Read the remainder of this chapter with an open mind and heart because if you do, I promise you will leave this chapter with a new perspective on the power of friendship as a foundation in romantic relationships. I am by no means suggesting that you must be friends with someone before you begin dating them. I am establishing a case that you must create time, space, and opportunity for friendship to grow between you and your romantic partner. A friendship foundation, or friends-first framework, is truly the difference between a tumultuous one-year relationship and a healthy and successful five-year relationship. The main source of strength you can pull from should a conflict arise is the friendship you have built with the love of your life. Why? Because love does not conquer all. We must have something more tangible, intimate, and meaningful first.

Let's spend some time discussing the components and processes surrounding friendships, which are, undoubtedly, the framework through which you should spark a romantic connection. Research has proven that it takes over 200 hours spent together as the necessary component for two people to become best friends, with 120 to 160 hours being the minimum for a close friendship to develop. Prior to that, two people must spend between 57 and 164 hours with one another to bridge the gap between acquaintances and casual friends within three weeks to three months. The research is clear that the time spent together must refer to actually being physically together in the same location. It does not include phone calls, FaceTime, or texting. The study concluded that at each interval, acquaintances, casual friends, close friends, and best friends, the number of hours needed to advance to the next level nearly doubled.

The relative timeframe also plays a role in friendship formation. Studies claim that close friendship is ultimately possible after 150 hours over ten days. This research highlights the importance and role of time in relationship formation. Those who invest more time are more likely to feel closer to their friend in question. The amount of time spent with another person contributes to a relationship's sense of intimacy. More time spent with another person results in the development of an enduring relationship, which ultimately satiates the need to belong. Hence the importance of frequent communication. Speaking often, checking in, and taking time to catch up are key to building intimacy. To keep good friends, you must spend time and effort investing in the relationship. I want to point out that you should, to some extent, disregard the consecutive days spent together because it's just not likely that we would spend that many consecutive days together for so many hours. Rather, I offered this research to prove that time, in terms of hours spent together, plays an imperative role in the development of friendship.

However, quality of interaction is not synonymous with quantity. While communication is important, small talk predicted a reduction in friendship closeness. Friendships that hinge on small talk result in lowered feelings of intimacy. Furthermore, what friends do during their time with one another is paramount. Time spent talking wasn't necessarily related to relationship closeness, meaning that the depth and content of a conversation are truly what change or advance the relationship. So please, stop asking potential friends or partners, "What's your favorite color?" Instead, dive a little deeper. Ask, "If you could change anything about your personality, good or bad, what would it be?"

Why Your Pattern Resists This

The friends-first path is not complicated in theory. In practice, your pattern will resist it. Specifically and predictably. Knowing how it will resist is the only way to stay in the process long enough for the friendship to actually form.

The Escapist mistakes the emotional availability that friendship requires for the same threat they feel in romance. The sustained presence, the deepening conversations, the slow accumulation of being known, the nervous system reads all of it as exposure. As risk. And so the Escapist begins to withdraw before the friendship is strong enough to become anything more. They leave before leaving is necessary and call it protecting themselves.

The Reactor mistakes the absence of intensity in friendship for the absence of interest. Friendship builds slowly. It is not cinematic. It does not arrive with the neurochemical surge that the Reactor's nervous system has been conditioned to read as love. So the Reactor either rushes past friendship into intensity, because intensity is the only thing that registers as real, or abandons the connection entirely as not enough.

The Rescuer builds a role instead of a friendship. They show up, they take care, they make themselves indispensable. And what develops is not a friendship between two equal people but a dynamic with the Rescuer at the center of someone else's needs, which is exactly where they learned love lives. By the time romance enters the picture, the imbalance is already built in.

The Skeptic tests the friendship. Not maliciously. Out of genuine self-protection. But the testing is thorough and relentless, and it exhausts people. By the time the Skeptic has accumulated enough evidence to extend trust, the other person has often already left.

The friends-first path does not fail because the idea is wrong. It fails because the pattern gets in the way before the friendship is solid enough to hold. Knowing this is how you choose differently.

Studies purport that friendship-based love, or compassionate, trust-based love, is still prevalent within romantic relationships and suggest that it might even be the basis by which we form romantic attraction. This is one of the key reasons why arranged marriages in certain Eastern cultures work so well. Instead of focusing on love first, couples focus on building a solid friendship, which then lays a fertile foundation that breeds intimacy, compassion, attraction, and ultimately, love. Western cultures idealize an illegitimate and highly romanticized definition of what love truly is. We want the perfect person, the ring, the beautiful wedding, the ability to call someone my husband or my wife, and the perfect married life. We view marriage as the end game, but the raw, unadulterated reality is that marriage is simply the beginning. And it is never perfect.

However, couples who have a higher rate of friendship-based love also report a higher rate of relationship satisfaction as it relates to affirmation and the degree to which we regard our partners. Ross and David are simply one example of this. Their mutual friendship is strong and meaningful, and they value it as highly as they do their romantic relationship. Furthermore, just like romantic relationships, friendships are mutual and reciprocal, particularly as they become closer.

Friendship love is much the same as romantic love, and the characteristics that bind you to your friends, like trust and positive experiences with one another, are replicated in a romantic setting. However, in the context of romantic relationships, friendship-based love is confounded by erotic love, or sexual attraction to the other person, which validates feelings of intimacy between the two participants.

The Components of Love

The foundation of friendship closeness is connected to love bonds usually found in romantic relationships. These bonds foster and strengthen neurological pathways to deepen intimacy. Love, according to relationship science, consists of three parts: intimacy, passion, and commitment. There are, of course, other factors that play a role in who and why we love, but largely, these are the components of the love you feel for anyone, regardless of romantic involvement.

Intimacy is widely considered to be the basis of love. Intimacy refers to feelings of closeness between two partners, or their bond with one another. Intimacy also refers to a desire to protect and promote a person's well-being, positive memories and experiences, high regard for the loved one, the ability to count on the loved one in times of need, emotional support, sharing, and valuing the person's role in your life. Intimacy is largely emotional and often follows a sort of script within a relationship. Early in a relationship's development, there will be a high degree of uncertainty which appears as stress, because one has not yet become able to predict the other's actions, emotions, motivations, and cognitions. As two people come to know one another, intimacy becomes more predictable and dependable. Intimacy is understood to be relatively stable in romantic relationships, as is commitment. In other words, intimacy and commitment are and should be constant for long-term relationship success. Furthermore, you have agency over your choice to be intimate with another person, and how you cultivate that intimacy.

This is the evidence I refer to when I speak to audiences around the world. I am known for stating: love isn't something that just happens to us. It is rather something that we allow to happen. We do not fall in love. We allow ourselves to choose love by being open and vulnerable enough to let love in.

Self-disclosure, or the habit of sharing personal information about your feelings, thoughts, or facts about yourself, is known to build intimacy. Additionally, intimacy is developed through a partner's response, particularly when we interpret their response as understanding and validating. However, simply sharing facts about yourself, like where you were born or your favorite color, is insufficient to build true intimacy. Emotional self-disclosure is thought to be more important to developing intimacy, as it allows an increased opportunity for our potential partners to make us feel validated and heard. Therefore, it is not solely the act of sharing information about oneself that is important. It is the content of the information shared, coupled with the partner's reaction, that is important in the development of intimacy.

Let's connect it: if self-disclosure, communication, and time spent together increase closeness on the friendship level, and those things are also the building blocks that lead to intimacy, both platonic and romantic, then we can confidently conclude that to have a healthy and successful relationship, intimacy first demands friendship.

Passion refers to the romantic or attraction component of love. Passion is widely understood to mean sexual tension or attraction between two romantic partners. In platonic friendships, passion may manifest as a strong emotional connection, a deep and abiding interest in each other's lives, or a shared sense of purpose or mission. It might also involve a sense of playfulness, adventure, or excitement in the time spent together, as well as a willingness to support each other through difficult times and challenges. In romantic relationships, passion goes hand in hand with motivation. We're subconsciously motivated to sustain a sexual relationship with those we find physically attractive, and oftentimes it is not exactly a choice.

However, passion goes beyond sexual desire. Passion satisfies our needs for validation and self-esteem, as well as self-actualization. Passion and intimacy are highly related to one another. Intimacy might arouse one's passion for another person. It is possible for two close friends to find themselves developing a physical attraction for each other that did not develop immediately and indeed did not develop until they achieved a certain level of intimacy with each other. Passion, though, is often quick to fade, particularly in long-term romantic relationships. At the beginning of a relationship, passion is high. Think great foreplay, stimulating conversations, and long nights. After a relationship extends past the honeymoon stage, passion usually subsides or decreases. Work is needed to maintain it.

Let's connect it: passion is the fuel that ignites intimacy's fire. In other words, passion is our physical response to intimacy. When you develop a closeness through friendship to foster true intimacy and combine that with compassionate passion, the connection you build will be deeper, more resilient, and more open than anything built on chemistry alone.

Commitment is the decision one makes to love someone and to be with them long-term. Commitment is considered to be what keeps the relationship going and is paramount to surviving times of difference and turmoil. However, the decision to love someone and the decision to commit to them is much different. It's ultimately possible to decide you love someone but similarly see no desire to be with them long-term.

In short-term romantic relationships, passion plays a large role in the relationship's foundation, and intimacy and commitment may play a minimal if not nonexistent role. In the context of long-term romantic relationships, passion may play a smaller role, and intimacy and commitment are more prominent. Commitment starts at zero before increasing rapidly in long-term relationships. Commitment is derived from the other two components of love. When we become intimate with another and value their well-being, we're motivated to commit to them in a long-term setting.

Let's connect it: commitment in friendship and commitment in a relationship are not mutually exclusive. You can commit to friendship but realize that a romantic relationship isn't for you. Do not allow the pursuit of romance to lessen or damage your friendship with another person. Both of you should simply agree that it's better to stay friends than it would be to pursue a romantic relationship.

Friends First, Lovers Later

Many people falsely believe that romantic partners cannot first be platonic. Our beliefs regarding relationship formation, particularly in the "men and women cannot be friends" ideology, stem from widespread heterosexism. Assuming that men and women cannot be platonic friends because sexual attraction permeates the relationship, and that all of us desire romance over platonic attachments, are types of biases that show up both culturally and in research settings.

The research resoundingly shows that most romantic partners begin as friends, or with a friends-first interaction before turning romantic. This model is most common in same-sex couples and in younger couples, particularly married couples under the age of thirty. Not only is this method prevalent, but studies illustrate it to be the preferred method of relationship formation, particularly in younger age groups. Therefore, it is ultimately possible and common for both heterosexual and LGBTQIA+ couples to first meet as friends.

I want to be honest with you about something here, because it's relevant and I think it will land differently coming from someone who has lived it rather than just studied it.

I have had friendships with women where, over time, it became clear that one person had developed feelings the other hadn't. I've seen these situations play out in my own life, and I've seen them play out in my clients' lives too. I've also seen the painful version where someone uses the guise of friendship to position themselves for a romantic opportunity they have no right to pursue. I experienced it firsthand in a relationship where a partner's close male friend worked consistently to undermine what we had and waited for what he perceived as his moment. I won't dramatize it further than that because that's not the point of telling you. The point is this: the reason I know these situations exist is the same reason I know they are the exception, not the rule. I have female friends I consider sisters. I would never cross a line with them. The friendship is the thing. Not what it might become.

What I want you to take from this is not that cross-gender friendships are dangerous. They are not. But, intentions matter, and healthy friendships require the same honesty and respect that healthy relationships require. If you are someone's friend while privately hoping they will eventually choose you, that is not friendship. That is waiting with a hidden agenda, and it will damage both the friendship and the relationship when it surfaces. Be honest with yourself about what you want. Be honest with the other person. And if the answer is that you want the friendship more than the romance, honor that. It's enough.

Research shows that most romantic partners begin as friends, and this research extends to people of all genders and orientations. The friends-first path is not a fallback. For many couples, it is the foundation that makes everything else possible.

All in all, there are multiple different ways we befriend others, but the ways by which we form close relationships are much the same. Relationships need time to develop, intimacy to strengthen the couple's bond, passion to maintain attraction, and commitment in times of turmoil. Without these, there is no love at all.

Before we go further

I want to give you the operating system for everything in this section.

It has three words. Responsibility. Regulation. Repair.

This is the Re/Model Lens™. It is not a communication strategy. Communication strategies give you scripts for the surface. The Lens gives you a framework for what sits underneath the surface and it governs everything in Phase 2.

Responsibility means owning your pattern's contribution to what breaks down. Not blame. Not shame. Clear-eyed accountability for what your nervous system does when it is activated, and what that costs the person across from you. The Escapist's withdrawal. The Reactor's escalation. The Rescuer's martyrdom. The Skeptic's testing. These are not character flaws. They are patterns. And owning them is not the same as being defeated by them.

Regulation means developing the capacity to manage your own nervous system before asking your partner to manage theirs. You cannot repair from a place of activation. You cannot recalibrate a connection while the pattern is still running. Regulation is the non-negotiable prerequisite — the step that has to happen before anything else in Phase 2 works. The Reset Ritual from Chapter 8 is your primary regulation tool. Use it before the conversations that matter.

Repair is the deliberate, skilled act of restoring connection after rupture. Not pretending the rupture did not happen. Not over-explaining or over-apologizing until the other person is managing your guilt instead of their own hurt. Moving through a specific sequence — responsibility named, regulation practiced, repair initiated — that closes the wound rather than reopening it.

These three words are the spine of Sections III and IV. Every chapter that follows is an application of one or more of them. Learn the sequence. It will become the most useful thing you take from this book.

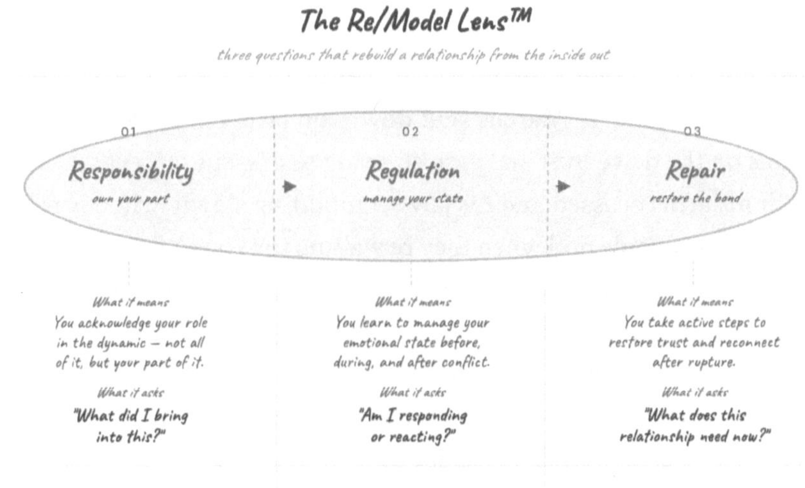

How Healthy Couples Fight

"Issues and conflict will arise in every relationship. But in healthy relationships, the deeper issue is recognized, and we work to chip away at it, moving from rupture to repair." — Esther Perel

Marcus and Diane had been together for six years when they came to see me. By the time they sat down in my office, they'd already decided the problem. Diane talked too much. Marcus shut down too fast. They'd rehearsed their positions on the drive over and arrived ready to present their cases. Marcus sat with his arms crossed and his jaw set, nodding slowly whenever Diane spoke, the way people nod when they're waiting for you to finish rather than actually listening. Diane spoke quickly, filling every pause before it could become silence, because silence, she'd learned, meant Marcus had already left the conversation even if his body was still in the room.

I let them go for about ten minutes. Then I asked them both to stop.

"What are you actually fighting about?" I asked.

They looked at each other. Then back at me.

"Communication," Diane said.

"What specifically?" I pressed.

She paused. "He makes me feel like I don't matter."

Marcus uncrossed his arms. His jaw softened just slightly. That was the real thing. Not communication. Not talking too much or shutting down too fast. The real thing was that Diane needed to feel like she mattered to the person she'd chosen to build her life with, and somewhere along the way, Marcus had stopped making her feel that way, and neither of them had known how to say it plainly until that moment.

That's what conflict does when it's handled well. It reveals what's actually there.

Recall the last fight you had with your partner. What happened? What were the main issues? Were there any specific triggers or events that escalated the argument? Now look at your own role in the fight. How did you contribute to its intensity? Did you purposely use any specific words, criticisms, or sarcasm knowing they would be hurtful? Were you aggressive? Accommodating? And finally, did either of you attempt to de-escalate or find a resolution during the argument? What steps have you and your partner taken to prevent similar fights from occurring in the future?

Many people believe they handle conflict well, or at least reasonably so. However, mitigating conflict is not synonymous with handling or managing conflict. I've found throughout my years of practice that few people truly understand relationship conflict, and those who believe they handle conflict with ease are often those who are most confounded by the concept. So before you continue reading, I ask you to take a moment to examine the way you approach conflict in your relationship by reflecting on the questions above. If you answer objectively and honestly, you'll likely find yourself wanting to make changes. It's okay to begin shifting what you believe about yourself and how you deal with conflict.

What Is Conflict?

Relationship conflicts are inevitable. All couples experience conflict in their relationship. Conflict consists of four elements: behaviors that instigate conflict, behaviors that perpetuate the conflict, behaviors that resolve the conflict, and the conflict's outcome. Conflict is not inherently negative and can allow a time to focus on relationship needs, partner needs, and the benefits of staying together. Conflict can be a productive way to address issues, and when effectively managed, can foster understanding, intimacy, and respect for one another. It often reveals issues, offers collective solutions, and boosts intimacy and relationship pleasure. However, it is not the amount of conflict that is detrimental to the relationship, but instead, how that conflict is managed and resolved. Conflict, in many cases, can be a sign of a healthy relationship, as it shows that both partners care about the relationship enough to invest precious time and energy into resolving their differences.

However, many of us enter relationships with the belief that conflict is negative and that it should be avoided. These beliefs are absolutely irrational and rigid. Believing that conflict is negative and must be avoided causes individuals to make impossible and unrealistic demands for the self, others, or the world, which cannot be met, and these beliefs lead to dysfunctional emotions and behavior. We believe conflict is negative because we live in a culture of good vibes, comfort, and fake successful relationships. We're constantly bombarded with images of healthy relationships, but don't let influencers' photos from vacations and social events fool you. All relationships have an inherent degree of conflict, but we are made to believe that love comes with constant agreement. Because of this, conflicts are seen as an insult or a lack of love and feel like they threaten the relationship's autonomy.

The belief that conflict is inherently negative can be detrimental in and of itself. This idea lessens positive and honest communication between individuals and leads to postponing, coercing, or deceiving a partner. Other irrational beliefs such as "I expect my partner to read my mind," "My partner cannot change," and "Men and women are just different" are also detrimental to conflict resolution. These false and misguided beliefs are associated with poor communication, lower relationship satisfaction, the prevalence of emotional and physical abuse, and a shorter relationship span. These beliefs perpetuate the notion that relationships shouldn't experience conflict, which is hindering you from unlocking your and your partner's potential for relationship success. You and your partner are two different people, and it would be silly to conclude that the two of you will never disagree about anything. Relationships should and do involve conflict, but how you navigate this conflict can determine the relationship's propensity for success.

The belief that partners should read one another's minds sounds crazy, and it is, but it is much more widespread than you might initially believe. In hundreds of coaching sessions and during Q&A after my speeches and workshops, audience members around the world reiterate this same statement. Many people believe that partners should understand their needs without verbal communication. However, this belief simply leads to disappointment, and research shows that those adopting this belief tend to behave in a hostile and combative way when a partner fails to sense their needs. A belief that the genders are fundamentally different operates from the misguided principle that men and women differ in their needs. This is far from the case and leads to lower relationship satisfaction and reduced sexual pleasure. Yes, you read that right. Unresolved conflict decreases sexual pleasure. Lastly, the belief that people cannot change is similarly dysfunctional as it eliminates a partner's hope for improving their relationship. Those who believe this have an external locus of control and feel that conflict's outcome is simply chance or circumstance. In believing this, people feel as though their behavior does not play a role in either conflict nor conflict resolution. You play a role in relationship conflict, regardless of whether you believe you're right or wrong.

Here is something worth sitting with: feelings are not facts. This perception often arises from the intense emotions one experiences during a heated situation. If someone feels that their partner doesn't care about them based on their emotional state, they may conclude that this is an undeniable fact. The importance of recognizing that feelings and interpretations can be subjective and influenced by personal biases, past experiences, and individual perspectives cannot be overstated. Just because someone feels a certain way doesn't necessarily mean it corresponds to an objective truth about the other person's intentions or character. In such situations, it's beneficial to practice empathy and open communication. Instead of assuming the other person's intentions based solely on your own feelings, it can be helpful to express your emotions and perceptions while also remaining open to understanding their perspective. This allows for a more balanced and constructive conversation where both parties can work toward a better understanding of each other's experiences.

Now that we've dispelled some preconceived notions about conflict, let's discuss positive conflict and its key components. Empathy is among these. Empathy, in this context, refers to the perception of emotions, changing one's perspective, and emotional responsiveness. Largely due to differences in socialization experiences, women are more empathetic than men on average. Nevertheless, empathy is needed equally to maintain and execute positive conflict resolution. Perspective-taking and certain empathetic behaviors have been found to be positively associated with good conflict outcomes and approaches. Verbal communication, or its strategies, are of the utmost importance for those navigating conflict. Verbal communication is integral to relationship satisfaction as a whole, as sharing information is among the key indicators and building blocks of empathy.

The future of your relationship is dependent on how you handle conflict. Couples must approach the conflict with curiosity and openness as opposed to defensiveness and blame. You must be willing to listen to the other person's perspective, even if it is drastically different from your own. And in doing so, you'll learn to be open to possibility, or to gaining a different perspective on the conflict at hand. Conflict is not a detriment but it is a predictor of relationship satisfaction. How you choose to navigate it, however, certainly is.

What Do We Fight About?

Understanding how, why, and when couples fight is paramount in a discussion about conflict and how it must be resolved. A study published in 1928 revealed that couples fought about personal habits, such as alcohol use, extravagance, frugality, mental issues, nagging, and anger issues, as well as topics focused on navigating a partnership, such as family interference, children, and outside companions. Nearly a century later, studies show that couples still fight about similar things.

According to a study published by the Journal of Family Issues, most couples fight about the following issues, ordered by frequency: communication, personal and partner habits, finances, decision-making, parenting, quality time together, sex, screen time, role expectations, time management, in-laws, employment and work expectations, food and meal choice, pet care, entertainment choices, gender roles, former partners, religion, and politics.

What couples fight about varies greatly by life stage. Parents fought most often about parenting, and couples in civil unions were more likely to argue about their in-laws, religion, and politics. In early marriage and young couples, arguments about finances, sexual intimacy, screen time, and emotional closeness were more common. Health and meal choices were more common in older couples. While conflict can play a role in relationship dissatisfaction, not all of these topics led to this conclusion. Arguments about sex, child-rearing, and finances correlate to divorce potential and relationship dissatisfaction. Couples who argue about chores and time management were actually happier than their counterparts, likely because these topics can be depersonalized. It's unlikely a reasonable person would take not doing the laundry as a personal attack. Finances and sex are a little more sensitive, as one considers sex to be a barometer for emotional intimacy.

Screen time is a large concern and component of many conflicts within the context of romantic relationships across age and relationship stages. Communicating online is associated with reduced relationship satisfaction and emotional closeness. We discussed this extensively in the Social Media chapter. Couples who divert their attention to online sources experience dissatisfaction, as this is time diverted away from their partner. So the next time you or your partner complain about screen time usage, understand that the underlying issue is not the fact that you're on the phone. It's that you are neglecting them, not spending quality time with them, and ignoring their attention needs.

Nevertheless, couples fight for a variety of reasons, and many of these reasons can be explained by attachment theory. Those with an **insecure attachment style** often adopt destructive conflict resolution strategies and report conflict based on their desire to provide their partner emotional and physical support, care, and direct attention. These people fear rejection by their partners, and to them, rejection and conflict are synonymous.

Because of this, they withdraw from conflicts, ignoring them altogether. Those with an **avoidant attachment style** engage in similar behaviors but tend to be poor communicators and distance themselves from the conflict. Those with an **anxious attachment style** escalate the conflict to tell and show their partners how much they have hurt them. They're not open to communication or negotiation and neglect to analyze the cause of the conflict. Individuals with an **anxious-ambivalent attachment style** are incredibly emotional when handling conflict and try to cope with their deeply rooted insecurities by seeking warm relationships. They engage in cycles of love and anger, flying off the handle one moment and love-bombing the next. Those with this attachment style fear rejection above all, and most arguments they engage in are those bred out of this fear. These attachment cycles predict not only how we engage in conflict, but also what we argue about.

What Is Your Fighting Style?

It is important in this context to understand not only how and why conflict arises, but how we fight. How couples fight is largely rooted in conflict styles, and I'll briefly explain these further. The Thomas-Kilmann Conflict Mode Instrument explains an individual's reactions and responses to conflict. The five styles are Competing, Collaborating, Compromising, Avoiding, and Accommodating. You likely embody one or more of these, and many people move through a few of them throughout an argument.

The **Competing** style is just that, competitive, and the person using this style is uncooperative and focused solely on their own concerns and interests. Those who compete exert their power over another person to maintain their interests. **Collaborating**, or collaborators, see the other person's interests as well as their own and cooperate to find solutions that satisfy both people's needs. These people look beyond the argument in question and analyze what might be instigating the argument in the first place. **Compromisers** sit in the middle. They seek a solution to the issue but don't look beyond the argument itself. These people make quick decisions as to how to resolve a conflict and don't address any potential underlying issues. **Avoiding** refers to those who do not pursue another person's interests, and in this case, the individual does not pursue their own either, choosing merely to avoid the conflict in the first place. They withdraw from the volatile situation because they feel threatened. This conflict style is closely related to the avoidant attachment style we previously discussed. Lastly, those with an **Accommodating** conflict style pursue the other person's interests but not their own. They seek to accommodate or satiate the other person's needs to resolve conflict and sacrifice their own needs in the process.

Collaborators are most successful at navigating conflict, as they do so by addressing the underlying issues that may be instigating the conflict itself. However, all of these conflict styles are real and valid, and it is important to understand yours when engaging in a romantic relationship.

Here is what that taxonomy looks like when you run it through the Re/Model framework™.

The Reactor defaults to Competing. When the fear of being unseen activates, the conflict becomes about survival. Winning is not the goal so much as registering proving that what was felt is real and cannot be dismissed. The competitive style is not cruelty. It is a nervous system demanding acknowledgment with the only tool it was taught.

The Escapist defaults to Avoiding. Not because the issues do not matter but because the body reads conflict as the beginning of something unsafe. Withdrawal is regulation by another name except that withdrawal does not actually resolve anything. It defers it. And deferred conflict accumulates interest.

The Rescuer defaults to Accommodating. Keeping the peace is how the Rescuer learned to keep love. Sacrifice their own position, absorb the tension, make the other person comfortable. What looks like generosity is often fear. The fear that holding a position will cost them the connection.

The Skeptic oscillates between Competing and Avoiding. When they feel exposed, they retreat. When they feel dismissed, they advance hard, precise, and difficult to argue against. The pattern underneath both responses is the same: maintain control of the distance.

Your conflict style is not a fixed personality trait. It is your pattern's default setting under pressure. The Re/Model Lens™: Responsibility, Regulation, Repair - exists to give you a different option. I will explain the Lens in more detail shortly.

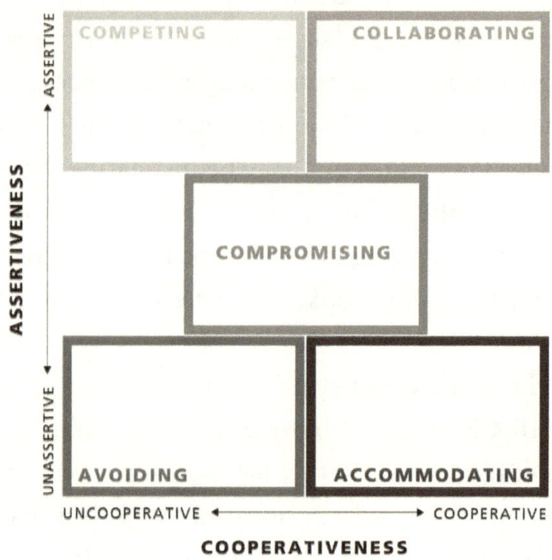

Ultimatums Do Not Work

Ultimatums, in any context but particularly in the context of romantic relationships, do not work. Most of us have relative familiarity with ultimatums. Maybe your parents used them to get you to do your chores growing up, or a previous partner slammed their keys on the counter and said, "Give up this or I'm leaving." Regardless of the situation, ultimatums are not a viable way to engage in conflict resolution, and nearly always lead to frustration and hurt from one or both parties.

Ultimatums are, at their core, a threat. Some perceive them as setting a boundary, but I vehemently disagree with this. Boundary setting is more comprehensive and compassionate, whereas ultimatums are definite and concrete. Ultimatums are mechanisms to control another's behavior, or to stack the odds in your favor. Boundaries, on the other hand, are rooted in the self. It is the difference between, "I'm no longer comfortable with this, and I'd like us to work on it," and, "Stop doing this or I'm packing." One of these statements, the former, is encouraging and helpful. There is a we being communicated. The other statement is definite and threatening. And for a person with an anxious attachment style, the latter statement can be devastating as it threatens the relationship altogether.

As we touched on earlier in the chapter, those with an anxious attachment style crave connection and acceptance from their partners, and this desire is bred from a childhood characterized by unmet emotional needs. This attachment style is, unfortunately, relatively common, and it is incredibly important to understand the styles of others so you may effectively resolve conflicts. Those with an anxious attachment style view ultimatums as threats and become resultantly distressed, perceiving them as abandonment. In response to ultimatums, those with this attachment style become sensitive to an anti-goal state, which in their minds is synonymous with abandonment. Those with this attachment style tend to accept more offers in order to be appreciated and are likely willing to accept ultimatums so as not to be left alone.5 However, in the case of manipulation and coercion, this can be used against those with this style, as the manipulator knows they can bend them to their will. This is not a healthy way to engage in conflict resolution, and coercion is never healthy. If you recognize that your partner is engaging in such manipulative behavior, leave immediately. I'll show you how to do this effectively in the final chapter.

Those with an avoidant attachment style avoid conflict as, to them, it is synonymous with rejection. They engage in behaviors that protect themselves from this as a means to avoid emotional turmoil. In the context of ultimatums, those with this attachment style provide low offers, and when they do provide ultimatums, they offer small ones. To those with this style, a large ultimatum, like leaving the relationship, is perceived as vulnerable, and rejection of this offer is thought to be a rejection of themselves.

Ultimatums only seek to threaten a relationship's foundation and eliminate important aspects of trust, communication, and understanding between two individuals. They may seem rather effective, but their efficacy lies in fear. Relationships and fear are mutually exclusive. You cannot engage in a healthy relationship if one partner fears the other's actions. Do not provide your partner with dangerous ultimatums. These direct, derogatory statements seek to harm both of you and, if you give them, more often than not, they'll backfire.

Call Your Partner "In" Before Calling Them "Out"

As we've established, conflict is an inevitable part of any romantic relationship, and the way couples handle their conflicts can either strengthen or weaken their bond. Disagreements, misunderstandings, and differences of opinion are simply bound to occur. The key to a healthy and successful relationship is not to avoid conflict but to handle it in a constructive and respectful manner.

Prior to discussing how we can implement effective conflict navigation strategies, we must discuss some key differences in how we approach conflict. To properly engage with a partner, we must first understand them. During arguments, in general, women tend to respond expressively, while men often respond negligently or avoidantly when resolving potential arguments. This is primarily due to social role theory. Individuals adopt certain stereotypes congruent with their perceived gender roles to face conflicts. Because of this, women's expression enhances their awareness and concern for their relationship, causing them to engage with the situation. Men, on the other hand, act in accordance with their stereotypical gender roles and may respond to conflict aggressively or avoidantly in congruence with their societally dictated roles. Men often adopt a facade of self-confidence during arguments, causing them to neglect and avoid conflict as they deem it threatening to their ego.

The way we engage with our emotions, or how in tune we are with our emotions and those of others, is what we call emotional intelligence. Emotional intelligence is a predictor of conflict resolution and relationship satisfaction. Both men and women who adopt effective conflict management strategies illustrate a higher sense of emotional intelligence, which in turn boosts psychological well-being. Women, contrary to popular belief, are no more skilled than men in regard to emotional intelligence. However, men's largely negative, aggressive emotional responses subjugate any sort of emotional connection during times of conflict and contribute to poor repair after conflict. Destigmatizing conflict resolution strategies is necessary to improve them. Gender and emotional intelligence are not related, but the ways we perform our genders play a role in conflict management. Emotional intelligence is among the key ways to successfully navigate conflict. Separate gender from the equation, and find satisfaction.

Showing emotional intelligence is a hallmark of the calling your partner in before calling them out method. This approach involves focusing on your partner's perspective and approaching them with empathy and understanding, as opposed to calling them out or placing blame on them for the conflict at hand. You and your partner are on the same team. It's you two versus the conflict.

This approach yields a variety of benefits. When we call our partner out, we focus on their behavior and its negative impact on us. We make it personal. This approach leads to defensive responses and feelings of being attacked. When we call our partner in, we approach the conflict with empathy and a desire to understand their perspective, which creates a safe and non-judgmental space for both individuals to express their thoughts and feelings without fear of being attacked. This approach also increases empathy between partners. When we call our partner in, we see the conflict from their perspective and labor to understand why they acted the way they did. This teaches us to develop empathy for our partners and their experiences, and this empathy leads to greater understanding, connection, and compassion within a relationship. When we understand our partner's perspective, we're better equipped to find solutions as a team.

Calling your partner in is much easier said than done. Here are some practical strategies you can use to try this technique.

Practice active listening. Active listening is an essential skill for this technique to be effective. Active listening involves paying close attention to your partner's words, tone, and body language. Body language comprises the majority of human communication and plays a pivotal role in conflict. Clarify what your partner is saying to you and reflect on their body language. If they're standing tall with open arms, mirror this back to them. This technique communicates understanding to your partner and shows them that you care about what they're saying. Active listening contributes to a supportive, safe space for communication.

Avoid blame and accusations. This approach can only be adopted by treating the argument as a team exercise, and by separating ourselves from the argument at hand. Blaming your partner puts them on the defensive and creates a hostile environment that isn't conducive to effective communication. Focus on using "I" statements to express how you feel.

Validate your partner's feelings. You might not understand how your partner feels, but that does not mean that what they are feeling is silly or invalid. Validating your partner's feelings refers to acknowledging and accepting their emotions, regardless of whether or not you agree with them. Validation creates a safe environment for communication and fosters mutual empathy and understanding.

Conflict is not inherently negative and is a normal and acceptable component of a healthy romantic relationship. It is highly unlikely that you and your partner will agree about everything. Certain topics lend themselves to less conflict than others, but successful resolution can often be found even within the most gut-wrenching, emotionally taxing arguments. Successful conflict navigation strategies are paramount to a healthy relationship. Blame, attack and defend cycles, and ultimatums are not among these. However, empathy, calling your partner in, addressing the root of the problem, and verbal communication certainly are.

Think back to Marcus and Diane. The moment the real thing surfaced, the conversation changed entirely. Not because either of them suddenly became better communicators, but because they stopped performing their positions and started telling the truth. That is what conflict, handled well, makes possible. It is not the enemy of your relationship. It is the doorway to the parts of it that actually need your attention.

Conflict is sure to occur, even within the most stable of relationships. You must navigate it together, not fight it or avoid it.

Avoid Attack and Defend Cycles

Attack and defend cycles are cyclical. One partner becomes angry and attacks the other for what happened. They may resort to name-calling or blame, degrading their partner and putting them on the defensive. The other partner becomes confused and sheepish, which eliminates empathy and understanding between the two. Attack and defend is a common conflict cycle, but it is not conducive to positive conflict resolution. To mitigate the effects of this cycle, you must use effective conflict strategies. Self-disclosure is a powerful way to redirect the conversation should a partner become defensive. Accepting responsibility is also highly effective and can mitigate the disdain and frustration the defending partner feels after the attack. The best way to avoid this cycle is to use a call-in technique, and we will further discuss this in the following section. Last-ditch efforts at redirecting the conversation are relatively ineffective and won't lead to two satisfied partners.

Conflict resolution strategies are well-established in the literature and primarily involve a few key stages.

1. Define the source of the conflict.
2. Explore and look beyond the initial incident.
3. Request and search for solutions.
4. Identify solutions that both participants can support.
5. Agreement and repair.

Repair is the stage most couples attempt and few complete. Not because they don't want to repair, most people want the rupture closed. But because repair requires a specific sequence, and most of us were never taught the sequence. We were taught to apologize. To make things better. To move past it. Those are intentions, not structure. And without structure, repair tends to reopen the wound instead of closing it.

The Three-Part Repair Structure gives the process what it needs.

1. **Name the rupture without relitigating it.** One sentence. What broke, stated without accusation or defense. Not "you always do this" and not "I can't believe what happened last night." Something precise: I felt dismissed when the conversation ended the way it did. The Reactor's challenge here is brevity, the body wants the full accounting, every grievance included. One sentence. The Rescuer's challenge is honesty, the pattern wants to apologize rather than name. Name what happened before you apologize for anything. The Skeptic's challenge is presence, stay in the room rather than retreating into analysis of what the rupture means about the relationship's future.

2. **Regulate before you reconnect.** This is the step most couples skip. Twenty minutes minimum. Neither partner attempts reconnection while the nervous system is still in activation. This is not the silent treatment. It is a structured pause. The difference is intent: the silent treatment is punishment, the pause is preparation. The Reset Ritual belongs here.

3. **Re-establish the friendship before you restate the conflict.** Before you return to the content of the argument, you return to the bond underneath it. A deliberate act that says: the rupture happened and we are still here. The Escapist needs to stay physically present during this step the pattern wants to treat the pause as an exit. The Reactor needs to lead with their voice low, not their position loud. The Rescuer needs to receive care here rather than give it, which will be uncomfortable. The Skeptic needs to say one true thing not a position, a feeling.

Repair is not the end of the conflict. It is the restoration of the foundation that makes the conflict resolvable.

When the System Fails: The Red Zone Protocol

Not every conflict stays in territory where the "call-in" technique is available. Not every escalation can be interrupted mid-flight. Sometimes both nervous systems have fully activated so the repair sequence is not accessible. Continuing the conversation will cause damage rather than produce resolution. This is the Red Zone. And the Red Zone has its own protocol.

Full stop. Both partners name, without blame, that the conversation has entered the Red Zone. I am in my pattern right now and continuing this conversation is going to make things worse. This is not giving up on the issue. It is protecting the repair process.

Twenty-four-hour hold. No re-engagement on the conflict for a minimum of twenty-four hours. Both partners use the Reset Ritual individually during that time. Not to prepare arguments. To regulate. There is a difference, and the pattern will try to blur it.

Re-entry agreement. Before the conversation resumes, both partners name one thing they are taking responsibility for. Not one thing the other person did wrong. One thing they own. The Reactor names the escalation. The Escapist names the withdrawal. The Rescuer names the martyrdom. The Skeptic names the test they ran. One thing. Stated plainly. Then the conversation can resume from a different starting position.

The Red Zone Protocol is not avoidance. Avoidance leaves the rupture open. The Protocol closes it temporarily and safely so that what needs to be said can be said by two people who are actually capable of hearing each other.

The Re/Model Lens™ applies here directly.

Responsibility in conflict means owning your pattern's contribution to the escalation not the argument's content, but the nervous system behavior that drove the temperature up. Before you address what the conflict is about, you name what your pattern did. Not defensively. Factually. My Reactor pattern escalated before I understood what you were actually saying. That is on me.

Regulation means using the Reset Ritual before attempting to call your partner in. You cannot call someone in from a state of activation. The call-in technique requires access to empathy, to perspective-taking, to genuine curiosity about the other person's experience. None of those are available when the nervous system is in threat mode. Regulate first. Then engage.

Repair is the third component of the Lens and the full subject of the next section is the sequence you follow after the heat has passed. Not immediately. Not while either nervous system is still running the conflict's energy. After.

Everything in this chapter: the call-in technique, the five stages of conflict resolution, the attack-and-defend interruption strategies is an expression of these three principles. The Lens is not an addition to the chapter. It is the framework the chapter is built inside.

Exercise: The Conflict Style and Pattern Audit:
www.carloshines.com/book/conflict-audit
or Scan the QR Code below

The Intimacy Gap

Renee and Marcus had been together for eleven years when they came to see me. They were not in crisis. That was the first thing they told me, almost defensively, as though admitting to a crisis would mean admitting to a failure they were not ready to name. They were fine, they said. Things were good. They just felt like something was missing and they could not put their finger on what it was.

It took about twenty minutes for me to put my finger on it.

They sat on opposite ends of the couch in my office with approximately eighteen inches of cushion between them. Not hostile inches. Not angry inches. Just inches. The kind of distance that accumulates so gradually you stop noticing it is there. They finished each other's sentences. They laughed at the same things. They had built a genuinely good life together, two kids, a house they loved, careers they were proud of, a friendship that was evident and real.

But when I asked them the last time they had been physically intimate with each other, they both looked at the floor.

"A while," Renee said.

"How long is a while?" I asked.

Marcus shifted in his seat. "Seven months, maybe eight."

Renee nodded. Neither of them looked at the other.

"And before that," I asked, "what did intimacy look like?"

They both paused in the way people pause when they are trying to remember something that used to be easy and has somehow become distant. Renee said, "It was good. It was really good." Marcus nodded again. "It was," he said. And then, quietly, almost to himself: "I don't know what happened."

I did. And by the end of our work together, so did they.

What happened was not unusual. What happened was not a sign that the relationship was broken or that the love had left. What happened was the intimacy gap, and it is one of the most common and least discussed dynamics in long-term relationships. It is the slow, almost imperceptible widening of the physical and emotional space between two people who still love each other, who are still committed to each other, and who have somehow, without meaning to and without noticing, stopped reaching for each other.

This chapter is about that gap. What causes it, what it means, and what it actually takes to close it.

What Intimacy Actually Is

Before we can talk about the gap, we have to be clear about what we mean by intimacy, because most people, when they hear the word, immediately think about sex. Sex is part of intimacy. It is an important part. But if you reduce intimacy to sex, you will spend your entire relationship trying to solve the wrong problem.

Intimacy is the experience of being fully known by another person and choosing to stay. It is the late-night conversation where you say the thing you have never said out loud and the other person does not flinch. It is the hand on the small of your back when you are standing in a room full of people and feeling completely alone. It is the inside joke that requires no explanation. It is the willingness to be seen without your armor on, in the bad moments and the boring moments and the moments where you are not performing anything for anyone.

Physical intimacy, what most of us call sex, is one expression of this. But it is downstream of the emotional intimacy that either feeds it or starves it. When couples come to me complaining that their sex life has deteriorated, what they are almost always describing is an intimacy gap that started long before anyone stopped reaching across the bed. The sex is the symptom.

The gap is the diagnosis.

Renee and Marcus had not stopped being physically intimate because they stopped wanting each other. They had stopped being physically intimate because they had stopped being emotionally intimate, so gradually and so naturally that neither of them had noticed it happening until the distance was already eighteen inches wide on a couch in my office.

How the Gap Forms

In Chapter 5 we talked about what dopamine does in the early stages of a relationship. The rush. The obsession. The way the other person occupies your every thought and the way your brain floods with pleasure every time they walk into a room. We also talked about what happens when the dopamine begins to settle, when the honeymoon phase gives way to something quieter and more sustainable, what scientists call compassionate love.

Here is what we did not fully address in that chapter. The transition from dopamine-driven passion to oxytocin-driven connection requires active participation. It does not happen automatically. And most couples, without realizing it, begin to coast at exactly the moment the relationship requires the most intentional investment.

In the early stages of a relationship, intimacy builds itself. You are learning each other. Everything is new. Every conversation reveals something. Every physical encounter carries the charge of discovery. Intimacy accrues almost effortlessly in that season because novelty is doing most of the work.

But novelty is not a renewable resource. And when it runs out, something has to replace it. That something is intention. Deliberate, conscious, sometimes inconvenient intention to keep reaching toward the person you chose, even when the choosing has become comfortable and the reaching requires effort you do not always feel like making.

Most couples do not make that shift consciously. Life intervenes. Work expands. Children arrive and consume every available hour. The mortgage and the schedules and the thousand small logistics of a shared life crowd out the space where intimacy used to live naturally. And because the relationship still functions, because the friendship is still there and the commitment is still there and the love is still real, neither partner notices that the intimacy has been slowly starving until one of them looks up one day and realizes they cannot remember the last time they truly connected.

That is the gap.

It does not form because love left. It forms because intimacy was never given a structure to sustain it after the early chemistry stopped doing the work for free.

How Your Pattern Widens the Gap

The gap does not form the same way in every relationship. How it widens depends on which pattern is in the room.

The Escapist creates distance through absence. Not physical absence. They are in the house, at the dinner table, in the bed. Relational absence. The emotional doors quietly shut one by one, so gradually that neither person notices until the distance is already wide. Their partner stops reaching because reaching stopped being received. The Escapist rarely intends the withdrawal. The pattern intends it for them.

The Reactor creates distance through temperature. The emotional intensity that felt magnetic in the early relationship eventually exhausts the safety that sustained intimacy requires. A nervous system that has been managing someone else's heat begins, eventually, to maintain distance simply to breathe. The Reactor's passion is real. The cost of it, over time, is also real.

The Rescuer creates distance through depletion. They give until there is nothing left of themselves to be intimate with, and then they wonder why the connection has gone quiet. Intimacy requires a self that is present. The Rescuer has spent so much energy attending to everyone else's presence that their own has thinned to almost nothing.

The Skeptic creates distance through managed access. They allow closeness but in controlled increments, at a pace they set, within limits they maintain. Their partner eventually stops trying to breach the distance, not out of disinterest but out of exhaustion. The Skeptic reads the withdrawal as confirmation that they were right not to trust fully. The loop closes.

The gap is not a sign that love left. It is a sign that the pattern was allowed to run longer than the intimacy could absorb.

The Emotional Before the Physical

I want to spend some time here on a dynamic I see in my practice more than almost any other, because it is the one that causes the most confusion and the most pain, and it is the one that is most consistently misdiagnosed.

When physical intimacy decreases in a long-term relationship, the partner who desires more of it almost always interprets the decrease as a statement about their desirability. He does not want me anymore. She is not attracted to me. I am not enough. This interpretation then produces behaviors, pressure, withdrawal, resentment, or performance, that make the intimacy gap wider rather than narrower.

What is almost never true is that the decrease in physical intimacy is actually about physical desire. What is almost always true is that one or both partners have accumulated a deficit of emotional intimacy that the body is simply reflecting.

Think about it this way. Emotional intimacy is the soil. Physical intimacy is what grows in it. When the soil is depleted, nothing grows regardless of how much you want it to. You can want the harvest all you like. If you have not been tending the soil, the harvest will not come.

What depletes the soil? Unresolved conflict. Criticism without repair. The slow accumulation of small moments where one partner reached and the other was not available, not because they were cruel but because they were distracted, tired, preoccupied, or simply unaware of how much that particular reach mattered. The absence of non-sexual physical affection, the hand-holding and the embraces and the small touches that say I see you and I choose you without requiring anything in return.

Renee told me in one of our individual sessions that she had stopped initiating sex not because she did not want Marcus but because she felt invisible to him in their daily life. He did not ask about her day. He did not notice when she was struggling. He was present in the house but absent in the relationship, and her body had simply stopped sending signals to a person who did not seem to be receiving them.

Marcus told me in his individual session that he had stopped initiating sex because every time he tried, Renee seemed distant and he did not know how to bridge the distance so he had stopped trying.

Two people. Both wanting connection. Both interpreting the other's withdrawal as evidence that the connection was no longer desired. Both wrong. Both right. And the gap between them getting wider every week because neither of them had the language or the framework to name what was actually happening.

This is the intimacy gap in action. And it is solvable. But not by addressing the sex first.

What Emotionally Intimate Couples Actually Do

I want to be specific here because specificity is where this conversation usually breaks down. When couples are told to work on emotional intimacy, they often nod and go home and have no idea what that actually means in practice. Let me tell you what it means in practice.

They bid for each other's attention and they respond to those bids.
Dr. John Gottman's research on what he calls bids for connection is among the most practically useful findings in relationship science. A bid is any attempt, large or small, to connect with your partner. It can be as small as pointing out something interesting outside the window, sharing a feeling about something that happened at work, reaching for your partner's hand during a movie, or making a joke and waiting to see if they laugh.

The response to the bid is everything. Partners who turn toward each other's bids, who receive the small reach and respond to it, build an emotional bank account that sustains the relationship through conflict, stress, and the inevitable seasons of distance. Partners who consistently miss the bids, who are too distracted or too withdrawn to notice them, slowly drain that account without realizing it.

By the time Renee stopped reaching for Marcus sexually, she had already stopped reaching for him in a dozen smaller ways, and he had stopped noticing those smaller reaches long before he noticed the absence of the larger one.

They protect non-sexual physical affection.

This one is simpler than it sounds and more powerful than most couples realize. Regular, non-sexual physical affection, kissing before leaving for work, holding hands while watching television, embracing without it being a prelude to something else, maintains the physical channel of connection even during periods when sexual frequency is lower.

When couples stop touching each other non-sexually, the only physical contact that remains is sexual, which raises the stakes of every physical encounter to a level that can make both partners avoid it. Sex becomes loaded with the pressure of being the only remaining form of physical connection, and that pressure kills desire faster than almost anything else.

Renee and Marcus had stopped touching each other casually. They had not decided to stop. It had simply stopped happening, incrementally, as the busyness of their lives consumed the small moments where it used to occur naturally. Reintroducing non-sexual touch before addressing sexual frequency was one of the first and most effective interventions in our work together.

They talk about sex directly.

This one is uncomfortable for most couples and essential for all of them. The couples with the healthiest sexual intimacy over the long term are not the ones with the most naturally compatible desires. They are the ones who can talk about their desires, their concerns, their preferences, and their disappointments without the conversation becoming a referendum on the other person's adequacy.

Most couples never have this conversation directly. They communicate about sex through behavior, through initiation and rejection, through mood and body language and the kind of silence that is louder than anything either of them could say. This indirect communication almost always produces misunderstanding, and misunderstanding produces the exactly wrong responses.

Talking about sex directly means saying what you want. It means asking what your partner wants. It means having the conversation about frequency and variety and what feels good and what has stopped feeling good without either person hearing the conversation as an accusation or a verdict on their worth as a partner.

This conversation is not a one-time event. It is an ongoing one. Desire changes. Life changes. What worked at thirty may not work at forty-two. The couples who navigate these changes successfully are the ones who talk about them as they happen rather than waiting until the silence has become so heavy it feels impossible to break.

SIDEBAR: The most intimate thing you can do for your relationship is say, out loud, what you actually need. Not what you think your partner wants to hear.

Rekindling Versus Rebuilding

Here is where I want to push back on some of the conventional wisdom in this space, because I pushed back on it briefly in Chapter 5 and I want to go deeper now.

Most couples therapy approaches to sexual and emotional intimacy are built around the concept of rekindling. Go back to what you had at the beginning. Recreate the conditions of early attraction. Remember what brought you together and return to it.

I understand the intention behind this approach. What I disagree with is the premise.

You cannot rekindle what you had at the beginning because the beginning was powered by dopamine, and dopamine does not return at the same intensity once the brain has normalized the relationship. The giddiness, the obsession, the way everything about the other person felt electric and new, these are not states you can recreate after years of shared life. And trying to recreate them places an unfair burden on both partners, who are not the same people they were at the beginning, and on the relationship itself, which has grown into something more complex and more real than it was in those early months.

What you can do, and what I believe is far more valuable, is rebuild. Not back to what you had, but forward toward something neither of you has had yet. A form of intimacy that is not powered by novelty but by genuine knowledge of each other, by the trust that has been built through years of choosing each other, by the specific and irreplaceable understanding that comes from having navigated hard things together and come out still standing side by side.

This kind of intimacy is quieter than the early passion. It does not feel like a roller coaster. It feels, in the best moments, like finally being in a room where the temperature is right. Like being fully known and fully chosen by someone who knows exactly what they are choosing.

Renee and Marcus did not need to go back to who they were at twenty-eight and thirty- one when they first fell in love. They needed to learn who they were now, at thirty-nine and forty-two, and find each other there. That is what rebuilding looks like. And it is available to any couple willing to do the work.

Rebuilding requires more than intention. It requires structure.

What Renee and Marcus discovered in our work together was not a new version of the chemistry they had at twenty-eight and thirty-one. That version was gone, and going back for it would have been chasing something neither of them could become again. What they built instead was something they had never had. A living structure for their connection. One that did not depend on chemistry doing the work for free, or on either of them knowing intuitively how to reach the other.

The Secure Connection Roadmap is that structure. Three components, built together.

Shared Relational Values. The five things the relationship must have for both partners to feel safe and seen. Not assumed. Not implied by ten years of history. Named. Written down. Agreed upon explicitly. Most couples have never done this. Most couples are operating on assumed values that were never verified which is how partners end up years into a relationship discovering they were building toward completely different things.

Relational Agreements. Specific, behavioral commitments that protect the shared values. Not rules imposed on each other. Agreements made by both, with full ownership from both. The distinction matters: rules create resentment because they feel external. Agreements create ownership because they feel chosen. The Rescuer's agreement will likely involve receiving care as well as giving it. The Escapist's agreement will likely involve committing to presence in specific, defined ways. The Reactor's will involve the Red Zone Protocol, practiced in advance, not improvised in crisis.

A Ninety-Day Intimacy Plan. A concrete, low-pressure structure for rebuilding physical and emotional intimacy in increments. Not a schedule. Not an obligation. A shared commitment to reaching toward each other in small, specific ways over a defined period — and to naming what works and adjusting what does not.

Renee and Marcus did not close the gap by wanting it badly enough. They closed it because they built a structure that made connection possible on the days when wanting was not enough.

At the end of this chapter, you will find the exercise on Secure Connection Roadmap. Use it to get an idea of how you've built a secure relationship structure.

When the Gap Is Too Wide

I want to say something here that does not always get said in books like this one, because I believe honesty is more useful than comfort.

Not every intimacy gap can be closed. Some gaps form because the relationship has fundamentally changed, because the two people in it have grown in directions that are no longer compatible, because the emotional injury accumulated over years has exceeded what repair can address, or because one or both partners have checked out in a way that predates any conversation about intimacy.

If you are reading this chapter and recognizing that the gap in your relationship has become something more than a season of disconnection, something that feels permanent and complete, please do not use this chapter as a reason to stay in something that is genuinely over. The goal of this chapter is not to convince you to save every relationship. It is to give you the tools to determine what you are actually dealing with.

A couple working through an intimacy gap, with both partners genuinely present and genuinely willing, is a couple that can rebuild. A couple where one partner has already left emotionally, even if they are still physically present, is a couple that needs a different conversation entirely. The chapter on breakups comes next. If that is where you are, it is waiting for you.

For everyone else, for the Renees and Marcuses who are still here, still invested, still sitting on the same couch even if there are eighteen inches of cushion between them, this work is worth doing.

Renee and Marcus closed the gap. Not all the way, not immediately, and not without discomfort. But they did the work. The last time I heard from them, they were planning a trip, just the two of them, the first one in six years. Marcus told me Renee had reached for his hand in the airport and he had held it the whole flight.

That is what rebuilt intimacy looks like. Not fireworks. A hand. Held the whole flight.

You've completed Phase 2!

Recalibrate the Connection. Three chapters. The friendship foundation that has to exist before romantic love can hold. The conflict navigation that moves toward truth instead of away from it. The intimacy structure that sustains connection when the chemistry stops doing the work for free.

You have been handed tools in each of these chapters. The Re/Model Lens. The Three-Part Repair Structure. The Red Zone Protocol. The Secure Connection Roadmap. These are not concepts to think about. They are instruments to use. The difference between the reader who finishes this book feeling inspired and the reader who finishes it changed is the decision to actually pick them up.

Phase 3 begins in Section IV. Accelerate the Results. Its job is not to fix what is broken. The broken things have been addressed. Phase 3 builds what neither of you has had yet. It starts with the hardest truth in the book: that before you can build something real, you have to be willing to grieve what you lost.

Exercise: The Secure Connection Roadmap:
https://go.carloshines.com/book/secure-connection-roadmap
or Scan the QR Code below

IV

Begin Again

Phase 3 begins in loss.
That is not an accident. Accelerate the Results does not mean move faster. It means move through more completely so that what you build next is not built on unprocessed grief and repeated patterns, but on the ground you have cleared by actually doing the work.
You cannot accelerate results you have not yet earned. This section is about earning them.

Broken by Love

Growing up, and well into my twenties, I'd lost so much in life.

At age eight, due to molestation, I'd lost my innocence. At twelve, I'd lost trust in my family. At fourteen, I lost my mom and her unrelenting love, lost my home, my sense of security, and living close to my cousins resultantly. In my late teens, I'd lost my sense of identity, my creative nature, and my will to love without conditions. In my twenties, I lost my marriage, friends, and material possessions. There were other relationships I lost but felt I should've held onto. At some point in my mid-twenties, I found myself in a place so dark and so consuming that I convinced myself that ending my life was the only way out of the pain. I know now that this was the voice of trauma talking, not truth. I got help. I kept going. But I want you to know that I've been in the kind of pain that makes you question everything, including whether you deserve to keep going. If you have ever been in that place, please know that you are not alone and that there is a way through it that doesn't require losing yourself.

I tell you all of this because loss has been one of my most persistent teachers. I felt as though I lived in a constant state of it, and loss itself became a self-fulfilling prophecy. The more I felt I was losing, the more I lived as if everything were already lost. This pattern extended to my romantic relationships. I anticipated, to the very second, when my partners would leave me, or when I would leave them.

I was all too familiar with loss, but no amount of previous heartbreak could have adequately prepared me for the profound impact of a relationship I entered years after my marriage ended. It shattered me to my core, causing a devastation that far surpassed any previous experiences. The weight of this breakup is unparalleled, and it seems unlikely that any future breakup could measure up. The overwhelming sense of loss consumed and descended upon me like an ominous cloud, engulfing my every thought and emotion.

I'd known for a long time that the relationship was no longer healthy and was realistically toxic in every sense of the word. But I tried everything to hold onto the memories from what we call the honeymoon stage. At the beginning, the relationship was exciting and blissful. Every day felt wrought with possibility. More than anything, I wanted to grasp those moments once more, though I knew deep in my heart that they were gone, and what was left was no longer serving what I wanted it to be. Have you ever been there?

Intuitively, we both knew the end was near. Our arguments were becoming more intense, meaner and nastier than usual. Sex dwindled to a screeching halt and by month six we'd stopped being intimate altogether. We no longer enjoyed being around one another as we had when we'd begun dating. Our mutual concern for one another's feelings faded. We'd begun to criticize everything the other person did. And the most telling of all: we only communicated when absolutely necessary. However, in many ways, I felt as though my heart wasn't ready for what my mind knew to be true. I wasn't yet ready to admit what my intrusive thoughts had been telling me for so many months. The end is near and approaching quickly.

Despite the glaring signs that pointed to the inevitable end of our relationship, I hesitated to bring it to a close, knowing all too well the immense pain that awaited regardless of the outcome. We went to church every Sunday, and each time, I'd pray to God, begging him to take away the feelings of love, attachment, and attraction I felt for her. I don't know what she prayed for as she stood next to me, but I pleaded with God, asking him, "Please give me the strength to leave this relationship. Please take away the love I have for her. Remove our connection. I just can't take it anymore. Give me a sign." At the time, I was a desperate soul fully aware that I didn't have the strength nor courage to brave another failed relationship, or better yet, another loss. Because for me, loss had started to look very much like failure.

Our last argument was the straw that broke the camel's back. And to this day, I'm still in awe of the fact that our last argument was small, petty, and seemingly inconsequential in the grand scheme of our decidedly toxic relationship. After that argument, my nerves were shot. Sweat was running off my body like a broken faucet turned on full blast. My heart beat from my chest, almost so loudly that I could hear it. I must've texted her a thousand times that night, but she never replied. I soon realized I'd taken her phone out of spite. I wasn't thinking clearly, and I didn't think that through at the time. In some strange way, it helped. I couldn't contact her, and she couldn't contact me.

But the prayers I'd whispered came true in a way that I wasn't quite expecting. I was prepared to grieve, but what I experienced was nowhere close to what I thought I'd prepared for. In the hours immediately following our breakup, I wasn't expecting an immediate response of emotional pain, confusion, or the physiological response to my mental anguish. I wasn't prepared for the sleepless nights nor the disturbed thought process of not being able to function. All I could think about was her. But incongruously, the very thought of her made me sick to my stomach. I'd ignorantly presumed that the hurt would creep up, or at the very least, that my emotions would tell me they were about to implode. This did not happen. I'd mistakenly believed I'd have time to prepare for the loss I experienced, but it washed over me like an immediate, unwelcome tidal wave. I was drowning in grief.

Unexpected Grief

Shortly after the breakup, I walked thirteen miles around the city. I was in a state of complete disillusionment, crying and praying. I kept repeating, "I'm love broken," to myself, and I remember feeling as though my heart was shattered. I couldn't breathe. Looking back at the walk, I don't remember much of anything. Not my surroundings, not where I had planned to go, not the physical exhaustion, not how long it took me to arrive at my best friend's house. Nothing. I do remember, however, the emotional distress. The nagging, aching feeling of my heart being broken. I felt this way for weeks. My body's physical response to a broken heart was real, and I could feel every crack. My nerves seemed to tremble endlessly. My heart palpitated like it was in atrial fibrillation, a type of irregular heart rhythm characterized by rapid and disorganized electrical signals in the top chambers of the heart. My brain went into overdrive. I couldn't eat. My stomach was upset due to anxiety, and I'd suddenly find myself in the bathroom crying and throwing up. It was surreal. No matter what I did, I couldn't for the life of me escape or stave off these feelings.

In the aftermath, I came to realize that I was suffering from situational depression, also called reactive depression. This is a type of adjustment disorder characterized by a depressed mood, a type of depression that occurs as a reaction to a specific stressful event or situation. A key distinction between situational depression and other diagnoses is its connection to a particular trigger or life event, such as the death of a loved one, the end of a relationship, the loss of a job, financial difficulties, or a significant life change. It's characterized by symptoms similar to those of major depressive disorder, such as prolonged feelings of sadness, hopelessness, and a loss of interest in formerly enjoyable activities. The symptoms of situational depression typically emerge within three months of the triggering event and improve as the person adjusts and copes with the situation. It is important to note that situational depression is in most cases temporary, lasting from a few weeks to a few months. However, if you're experiencing symptoms that persist or worsen over an extended period, please seek professional help from a mental health provider for proper evaluation and support.

It took six months to get back to my former self. During that process, I came to realize that grief is incredibly sneaky, creeping up on the griever unexpectedly and oftentimes, undesirably. A sound, a smell, a glance, a song, all had the power to reduce me to tears even in the happiest of moments. Grieving a romantic partner is among the hardest battles we must overcome, but it can be done.

Our minds, bodies, and feelings don't understand the difference between the death of a loved one and a broken attachment. The brain views these events as entirely the same. My body was responding to the loss of an attachment, as though someone I'd loved dearly had died. Post-breakup grief is real and tangible, much like the grief one experiences after the loss of a loved one.

How Your Pattern Grieves

Grief does not arrive the same way for everyone. Your pattern does not disappear when a relationship ends. It becomes your grieving strategy. Knowing how it operates is how you stop letting it also become your avoidance strategy.

The Escapist goes quiet. Not because the grief is not present, it is fully present, exactly as real as anyone else's. But the pattern suppresses its expression so effectively that the Escapist appears fine. Functions normally. Moves through the world intact. The wound stays open underneath the performance of okay for months, sometimes years, until something small finally breaks through what the pattern has been holding together. The Escapist's risk is never actually processing what happened, because processing requires the emotional availability the pattern has spent a lifetime restricting.

The Reactor grieves out loud and cyclically. The feelings arrive at full volume and in full view. The processing is visible and thorough and genuine. The problem is the cycle the grief spikes, subsides, spikes again, and the settling that actual healing requires never quite comes. The Reactor's risk is re-traumatizing themselves and everyone around them by cycling through the loss so persistently that it cannot complete.

The Rescuer redirects. The grief is real, but the pattern converts it into action taking care of friends, being there for family, showing up for everyone who needs them while their own wound stays untended. Care without self is the Rescuer's default, and grief does not change that default. It just gives it a new context. Their wound stays open because tending it would require receiving care rather than giving it. And receiving care is exactly the thing the Rescuer has never quite learned how to do.

The Skeptic analyzes. They understand with crystalline clarity what went wrong, why it happened, who was responsible, and what it means about relationships in general and this one specifically. The intellectual processing is thorough and often genuinely insightful. The emotional processing lags far behind. The Skeptic achieves understanding without ever quite arriving at feeling which means the wound closes over without fully healing, and the next relationship inherits everything the analysis never reached.

Your pattern does not protect you from grief. It shapes how you avoid it. Knowing this is the beginning of actually moving through it.

Grief, Society and Attachment

For centuries, humans have been dealing with grief as an abstract and unwelcome stage of life. During the Victorian Era, grief was systemic and ritualized, allowing the griever adequate time to properly heal from their deep loss over a one to three year period. Unfortunately, today, though scientists and researchers have found strong similarities between the grief of losing a loved one and the emotions and physical experiences one endures after the loss of an attachment, we do not treat the two events similarly, even though our brain does. I'm not suggesting you wear black for two years after a breakup. I'm merely pointing out society's linguistic and behavioral dissonance in grief and loss. Grief and loss, and the feelings that comprise them, are legitimate and valid feelings that everyone, regardless of their circumstances, will experience. Your grief and mine, as complicated, conflicting, and antagonizing as it may be, were over the loss of an attachment, and that is valid in and of itself.

Much, if not all, of our ideas about breakups hinge on socialization, and this extends to our ideas of happily ever after. As we discussed extensively in Chapter 1, happily ever after is a fever dream, and this notion has little viability in our modern reality. As society's perceptions of relationships shift to a less patriarchal, more comprehensive model, our ideas about happily ever after lag. A century ago, it was common to marry the boy next door, or your first partner. Buying a house in the suburbs with a white picket fence with the person with whom you shared your first kiss was commonplace. As our world becomes more global and interconnected, this is no longer common or feasible. Statistics show that most people fall in love three times over the course of their life, and I'd argue that this number is realistically much higher. People engage in between five and ten romantic relationships over the course of a lifetime on average, and this number is on the rise. It's unlikely that all but one or two of these will end in happily ever after. Therefore, happily ever after isn't the reality we live in. Endings are. And our reactions to these endings are augmented as a result of socialization.

Contrary to popular belief, relationship dissolution is not a single, finite event, but a series of events, phases, or stages that gradually unfold. In most cases, that last fight, the fight of all fights, wasn't the end of your relationship. This was much the case for me and my worst breakup as well. The final fight was the last straw for both of us, and was the culmination of smaller arguments, events, and disillusionment we both could no longer ignore. Relationship dissolution is the process of learning that one should leave a relationship, or the process through which an individual realizes that leaving is best for their future. Dissolution is different from the breakup itself. Dissolution refers to the process of breaking up and begins long, sometimes months and years, before the final decision. Breakups, on the other hand, are the actual act of ending the relationship. It's that conversation where one individual tells their partner, "I just can't do this anymore." A variety of factors contribute to breakups and relationship dissolution, but both are the series of indiscretions, comments, arguments, or events that lead one person, or in the case of mutual breakups, both people, to decide to leave the relationship.

As humans, we have a strong desire and innate drive to make and maintain attachments with our romantic partners. The brain is hardwired to undergo this process. It creates neural maps for each of these and reminds us chemically that we love the individuals we have chosen. The brain also keeps track of our most important relationships along three dimensions: space, time, and depth of the connection. When we are separated, our brain keeps our bond intact by predicting when, where, and whether a reunion is likely to happen. These dimensions are also referred to as here, now, and close. For example, you implicitly know when your partner enters a room or when your beloved friend is at the door. So when you break one of these attachments, the brain tries to maintain its former connection to preserve its neural map. Changing this map is a large undertaking and requires a great deal of time to completely reroute. During that time, you may feel, see, or hear your loved one, because your brain is still holding onto here, now, and close, and you may feel disoriented and confused. It takes time and effort. Though you know your relationship has changed, your brain can't yet comprehend this information. In other words, breaking the attachments our bodies so laboriously work to make and maintain interrupts and subverts our natural inclinations, which causes a great deal of antagonizing stress and anxiety.

Neuropsychology explains why breaking up is such a difficult, emotionally overwrought process, but this doesn't make coping with breakups any easier. The feelings you encounter after a breakup, the anxiety, depression, and physical reactions, are tangible and real, and warrant addressing. In the aftermath of my breakup, I realized that the old saying time heals all wounds was a bald-faced lie. Time didn't heal me in the slightest. Hard work and conscious effort did. In fact, all of the sayings, colloquialisms, and advice I'd consumed felt stale and silly. Throughout my life, my friends had told me, "The best way to get over one partner is to get under a new one," but this too felt false. These pieces of advice are a crock of shit. If we entertain that particular route, all we're doing is suppressing our feelings and exchanging one addiction for another. It's much like vaping to get over smoking cigarettes. You're still damaging your lungs, just using a different vehicle to do it. Instead of this, take the time to heal yourself while being alone. We're no good in relationships if we keep entering them damaged and broken.

Shattering the Illusion

The approaches we choose when ending a relationship are dynamic and personal, but there are certain crucial factors that influence the manner in which we break up. To fully understand breakups and post-breakup grief, we must take into account a broader context, which includes the societal and cultural norms that shape our perceptions of love and loss, as well as the psychological concepts and emotions that intricately intertwine with and complicate our relationships.

As they grow up, children are exposed to ideas of love. We discussed the ways we learn about love in Chapter 1. Media, family, and other external processes falsely teach us how to engage in romantic relationships and serve as hallmarks of the socialization process. Disney movies such as Frozen, Cinderella, and Snow White support and define a child's definition of love. They grow up watching a beautiful princess attending balls, meeting Prince Charming, and riding off into the sunset. We learn that love is synonymous with happiness and acceptance, and this line of thought clouds our definition and ideas about what love should be. At family dinners and holidays, our parents scorn Great Aunt Mildred for never finding love, calling her a spinster or worse, and we internalize their message, learning that being single is less than favorable.

As we grow older and into our teen years, we're continuously exposed to ideas of love, and these ideas are no less harmful to our socialization. Teens watch their friends begin dating and, on social media, see pictures of their friends out on dates with captions that exclaim nervous excitement, and scroll past their elaborate prom proposals. TV shows present romance as inherently unhealthy and conflict-ridden, and as we subscribe to these images, we normalize them and believe that love should be wrought with drama and heartbreak.

What worries me most is that throughout all of these socialization processes, we've come to believe that we aren't worthy without romantic love, and I see the detrimental effects of this regularly. After all, how many happily single Disney Princesses and TV heroines can you think of? Go ahead, grab a pen. I'll wait. Zero. Why? Because we are socialized to believe that without romantic love, we are not wanted. Because we equate love to acceptance, we seek out romantic entanglements often and carelessly, leaving little room for anything else.

We believe we're nothing without love, and this notion mars the breakup process. When we encounter a breakup, we're not only met with the brain's neuropsychological response to the loss of an attachment, but we're left with complicated feelings of inadequacy and pain. This is why letting go is so difficult. We're attached to love as an emotional and biological process, and as a social one. Biologically, our brains are tasked with re-routing and changing their signaling. Socially, we have to face the fact that because we're without love, we're effectively unworthy. This is far from the case, and these ideas are doing nothing to help you through the loss of an attachment. Instead, they're complicating the natural process of breakups. We see singleness as the unknown, or a sad, lonely abyss, when it's truly an innate state of healing.

The decision to break up, as well as our perceptions of the process of breaking up, are complicated because of our misguided and false ideas about love. Breakup decisions are, at their core, decisions of whether to stay or leave. The person making the choice has to weigh the benefits of staying with their partner and compare these to the potential benefits and drawbacks of leaving them, and these drawbacks and our perceptions of them heavily hinge on our societal interpretation of love. Studies point to emotional intimacy, or feelings of closeness to a partner, as the most common reason for wanting to stay in a relationship. Logistical barriers such as financial barriers or cohabitation are among these reasons as well, suggesting that dependence is a common reason for staying with a romantic partner. Important issues such as infidelity, unmet emotional needs, and low sexual satisfaction are often the cause of breakups. Some factors, such as social pressures and consequences, validation and its lack, and self-improvement or self-hindrance, are listed as reasons why a person might either stay or leave a relationship.

The way individuals perceive, interpret, and process the imminent end of a relationship depends on their investment, gender, and role in the breakup. Investment, in this context, refers to the amount of time, selection, and resources the person has placed on and in their partner. Therefore, in response to the threat of a breakup, those who have invested more in a romantic relationship have a heightened perception of the cost of losing it. If a partner has put off their career goals, moved to a new city, or has spent ten years with a person, they will be more likely to avoid a breakup entirely. In response to the threat of breaking up, they go to great lengths to appease their partner, even if it means being unhappy. However, if these attempts fail, they may lash out and confront their partner, demanding to understand why they would want to leave the relationship.

Men in particular are prone to using lashing out as a behavioral strategy. Statistically, men are much more likely than women to turn their physical formidability against their mates as a tactic of mate-guarding, and this tactic can become volatile quickly. Women fear this intimidation and threat, so if the male partner threatens her emotionally, verbally, or physically, she may choose to stay in the relationship to stave off violence. Women, in general, have a stronger desire to maintain emotional intimacy within a relationship and actively seek partners who invest in them emotionally. Men, unlike women, when facing the threat of their relationship ending, may employ a strategy that exploits their partner's evolved preference for long-term mating. In response to their female partner disengaging, the male partner may attempt to keep his sexual access to a woman by increasing his emotional investment in her. Men threatened by a relationship ending may suggest they become exclusive to one another, cohabit, obtain a mutual pet, get married, or have children. Men are likely to increase their emotional investment in their female partners to manipulate their natural desire for emotional intimacy.

Women, on the other hand, often engage in the opposite behavior. When a woman sees her male partner disengaging from a relationship, she may make attempts to initiate sexual contact as a mechanism of reminding the male partner of her value. Women have told me that they used this mechanism in a variety of ways. They increase the frequency of sexual intercourse, they become more adventurous in the bedroom, and the saddest version I've ever heard was a woman trying to become every other woman her partner wanted her to be in an effort to maintain his attention, thereby losing herself in the process. None of these attempts is fruitful in most cases and often leads to increased hurt feelings during and following a breakup. Keep in mind that much of relationship research is heteronormative in nature. It is safe to say that these strategies can and are employed in same-sex couples as well, but the ways by which individuals perceive, place stock in, and engage in these behaviors vary.

During a breakup, the rejector, the person initiating the breakup, often begins using preemptive strategies, such as infidelity. Infidelity, in this context, operates on two principle ideas. It serves as a means of fulfilling the person's sexual and emotional needs, and as a way to end the relationship.

During the breakup itself, rejectees, the person being rejected or dumped, regardless of gender, investment, and other factors, often desire to maintain the relationship. Rejectors, regardless of the same influences, often reject their partner with the assumption that they can obtain a better mate or are better off without the existing mate. This difference can be explained in part by the better-than phenomenon. Humans are highly attached to their social perception and fear ridicule and shame following a breakup.

After the breakup, both parties are likely to experience a certain degree of anguish, sadness, and resentment. In general, however, rejectees experience more depression following a breakup than the person who rejected them. Rejectees are more likely to experience rumination over a breakup, as well as decreased self-esteem. During the breakup, the rejectee is likely to display a wide variety of behaviors, such as crying, pleading, and in some instances, threats of self-harm. Both parties, regardless of gender or role in the breakup, are likely to feel vengeful, angry, remorseful, and regretful after the breakup. Those rejected report higher degrees of sadness, confusion, anger, shock, and jealousy than their rejectors. Rejectors, on the other hand, experience greater feelings of both guilt and happiness.

So regardless of whether you're a rejector or rejectee, and regardless of gender, the ways by which we respond to breakups hinge on the way we as a culture perceive love and romantic attachment. Our idealized images of love overshadow our ability to make rational breakup decisions and cast a cloud over our grieving process. Letting go is difficult, and the decision to do so is complicated and dependent on a variety of factors, but it's no less doable. I urge you to remember that endings are natural and just as important as beginnings are.

The Art of Mourning: The Lowdown of Post-Breakup Grief

Anyone who's been broken up with knows this all too well. Breakups hurt. There's no better way to say it. Breakups, regardless of whether or not you were the rejector, hurt emotionally. Online blogs, social media threads, and articles preach the ins and outs of breakups, dissecting them and creating from them a science. However, as you read this section, I ask you to dispel any and all of the preconceived notions you have about what breakups should look like. There is no correct way, method, or timeline as to how and when you should heal from a breakup. Every relationship, person, and circumstance is different, and each person's healing process varies greatly. In fact, your breakup healing process might shift from relationship to relationship. But I urge you to heal on your own timeline and allow those around you to do the same.

Throughout history, humans have adhered to certain mourning traditions. Ancient Hindu practitioners would mourn the loss of a loved one for twelve days and then hold a feast to honor the deceased. Similarly, in China, immediate family members were expected to publicly mourn for forty days and refrain from wearing red. Mourning, historically, has been regarded as socially acceptable and a communal affair, with grief being recognized as a widely accepted emotion.

Although the term grief typically refers to the loss resulting from the death of a loved one, it can also encompass other types of loss, such as the end of a romantic relationship. Scientists have long recognized the connection and similarities between the grief experienced after a breakup and the grief experienced following the loss of a loved one. In fact, individuals often consider a breakup to be one of the most significant non-death-related loss events. As a result, breakups operate in a manner akin to the five stages of grief. This finding aligns with other research in the field of grief and loss.

When we are in love, our brain's reward system becomes activated, much like its response to drugs. Rejection, therefore, represents the loss of this love, and brain scans of individuals going through heartbreak bear resemblance to scans of those mourning the death of a loved one. Consequently, the body's response to a breakup closely mirrors its response to death, emphasizing the significant role of grief in the process of a breakup. Breakups can cause tangible, cognitive, and physical distress to individuals, regardless of their role in the dissolution of the relationship, and this distress is equally valid as the grief felt after the passing of a loved one.

Following a breakup, a wide range of symptoms can manifest. In my personal story, I felt physical symptoms of panic, coupled with a loss of appetite, feelings of emptiness and despair, lack of energy, irritability, and foggy thinking. Additionally, I went through crying spells and a loss of interest in activities I previously enjoyed. You might also experience shortness of breath, feelings of depersonalization, and bodily weakness. Emotionally, you may grapple with sadness, anger, guilt, helplessness, yearning, and anxiety, as well as certain cognitive symptoms, including the inability to concentrate, difficulty making decisions, and forgetfulness. Sleeplessness, insomnia, and intrusive thoughts are also common. After a breakup, you might feel a certain desire for the partner who rejected you, but this desire is often contradicted by your intense feelings of anger and sadness. That conflicting feeling confused me the most while I was going through my breakup.

The brain and body naturally respond to stress by secreting neurohormones in what is known as the fight or flight response. During times of stress, heart rate increases, pupils dilate, and the individual suffers from loss of appetite as a response to these hormones. All of these symptoms are normal and expected during the breakup process as your body changes and reacts to the stress and grief of losing someone you love. It is altogether common and normal for you to experience these symptoms intermittently.

You might feel fine for a few days, then find yourself lost in a hurricane of sadness and regret. Healing does not operate linearly, and you may find that yours is more sporadic and difficult to categorize. All of this is normal, and your emotions, as confusing as you may find them, warrant attention.

Many individuals experience intermittent and short-term bouts of low self-esteem and a lost sense of self directly following a breakup. Along this line, certain parts of the brain become activated during this process, including the risk-taking part of your brain. Everyone has a friend who copes with breakups disastrously. They get drunk, put on their tiniest dress, and end up across town in bed with a complete stranger. And they do this often, or at least until they've processed the breakup. Before you tell this friend to get over it, remember that their reaction is innate and biological. They are behaving in response to extreme stress and anxiety. Telling them to get over it is not motivating or helpful.

Certain variables, such as the individual's attachment style and perceived relationship closeness, are strong indicators of grief intensity in the context of breakups. The closer the two individuals are, the more intense their feelings of longing and loss are when they part ways. Closeness does not equate to longevity, however, and this is a generalization, not a hard and fast rule.

Attachment style is often predictive of an individual's response to a breakup because the concept of romantic love is seen as an attachment process, whereby individuals develop a reliance on their romantic partners as a source of emotional support and validation. Those with an insecure, anxious, or avoidant attachment style appraise stressful events such as loss as more threatening and are generally less competent to manage them than securely attached adults. Anxiously attached individuals exhibit more negative responses to breakups than those with a secure attachment style and are more likely to use drugs and alcohol to cope. They report higher levels of anxiety, depression, loss of behavioral and emotional control, and affect. This remains true for all genders and ages. Those who have an insecure attachment style respond to breakups less favorably. It is important to understand your attachment style and to comprehend how it affects your response to breakups. Therapy can be an incredibly powerful tool for coping with one's attachment style in the breakup process and its aftermath.

There are a wide variety of tips and hacks to help you navigate breakups, but these are often unsubstantiated and rooted in misguided social norms. I've heard certain rules for a timeline, short mathematical equations to explain when and how long a person should grieve, and even anecdotal evidence in favor of jumping back onto the dating scene as soon as the person leaves your apartment with their bags. This evidence and advice is deeply harmful and removes all elements of personalization and humanity from the grieving process.

Society doesn't emphasize post-breakup grief as it does grief experienced after a loss from death. We come to believe that breakups are less harmful and less difficult to navigate as a result. This isn't the case. The research points to breakups being just as emotionally and physically difficult as other types of loss. There is no one trick or hack to snap out of post-breakup grief, and the feelings you're experiencing are entirely valid regardless of your age, gender, or the type of relationship you're healing from. Post-breakup grief doesn't follow a specific timeline. You might move through all of grief's stages, denial, anger, bargaining, depression, and acceptance, in order, or you may jump to depression and move to acceptance before experiencing a breakup relapse. There is no perfect way to move through a breakup, but there are ways to help you through it.

Embracing the Void

We've discussed how breakups happen, the decision to break up, and the symptoms you're likely to experience as a result. However, within this uncomfortable and often emotionally draining process is a glimpse of hope, a reminder of the person you can be. One with new knowledge and self-discovery as a result of the breakup's aftermath.

Coupled with the symptoms and physical responses we laid out above, you're likely to experience feelings of emptiness and uncertainty. These feelings aggravate the healing process and are often the source of the low self-esteem and social disengagement you intermittently feel following a traumatic breakup. Breakups, particularly those with someone with whom you imagined a lifetime, come with an inherent degree of uncertainty. The life you'd imagined is gone, and you're left with the process of reimagining your own potential. As scary as this is, this process is full of possibility. Instead of acting out a narrative in which you were cast in a specific, even confining role, you have the opportunity to rewrite this narrative on your own terms and bend it to your will.

Sitting with this uncertainty can be daunting, and even paralyzing. In the days and weeks following your breakup, you'll likely experience a certain degree of situational depression, as I did following my own. And with this depression comes an inherent degree of loneliness and uncertainty. I need you to know that this is normal. And you will make it through this tough time. But instead of letting these feelings consume you, I propose another alternative: self-discovery. It's imperative, following a breakup, to rationalize the ways in which you and that person were not compatible, re-examine the red flags, think about the levels of toxicity, and seek to understand how you can use this information to heal. Do not beat yourself up about what happened. Instead, practice self-compassion for the person you were before today. Patience is needed to allow this process to effectively occur. Along that line, time doesn't heal wounds. You do. Consciously acknowledge what you're feeling, and reflect on why you might be feeling that way.

Einstein's definition of insanity is doing the same thing over and over and expecting new results. Breakups, and their aftermath, operate much like this. You can't expect to find yourself in a loving, healthy relationship if you continue engaging in the same, unhealthy patterns over and over again. So while breakups are difficult and uncomfortable, they offer you an opportunity to do things differently in the future. While you realize and rationalize what happened, I ask you to practically consider how you can take what you learned from your last relationship and apply it to the ones you engage in moving forward. What happened wasn't entirely your fault, or maybe it was, but breakups, much like mistakes, are opportunities to learn. Things do happen for a reason, and oftentimes that reason is designed to teach you a lesson, to force you to look at things differently, and more importantly, gives you the experience to be a better you.

I would recommend using the time you're single to evaluate and re-engage with those around you. Too often, when we are in relationships, we allow ourselves to become distant from those close to us because we want to give our romantic partners that time. This should never be the case, but I realize it's a reality. The establishment and maintenance of bonds are paramount. Surround yourself with loving, supportive people, and don't hesitate to rely on them for emotional support. These people are there to remind you that you're not alone, hapless, or unlovable. Spend quality time with those people and lean on them when you need a little extra help. Another one of my favorites is to reclaim your time. After a breakup, engage in new activities and exercises with the time you've freed from the relationship. Try activities that make you feel confident and positive about yourself. Exercise is among my favorites, but there are many ways to re-engage with yourself following the end of a relationship. Remind yourself that you're an individual worth loving. Use this time to reintroduce yourself to yourself.

In the intricate dance of love and loss, I unearthed a profound truth that defies conventional understanding: it is through the act of breaking that we find ourselves whole. In the aftermath of the relationship that followed my marriage, where I felt shattered and torn, I embarked on a journey of self-discovery. Paradoxically, it was in my brokenness that I discovered the hidden reservoirs of resilience within me. Like a phoenix rising from the ashes, I transformed my pain into strength, and my wounds into wisdom. It is within the depths of heartbreak that we uncover our truest selves, for it is in embracing our broken pieces that we discover the profound beauty of our own resilience.

The Hidden Gems of Loss

A good friend of mine recently endured a traumatic, horrible breakup, and came to me for advice. As we sat over coffee and charcuterie, we lamented her ex, who'd been overbearing, misogynistic, and manipulative. We discussed all of their troubles: the time he ripped up the photos she'd hung on their shared refrigerator, the time he told her to lose weight, and the ways he'd cheated on her throughout the latter half of their courtship. After the better part of two hours, she paused and looked at me for a moment, recalling a conversation she'd had with him the day before she left.

"He said he could make certain women fall in love with him," she paused, reclining for a moment, before looking out the window. "What did he mean by that?"

I too paused, purposely using silence as a tool for awareness. "I think the key phrase here is certain women," I said, looking at her. I wasn't going to tell her the truth just yet, so I paused again. I'd planned to let her come to her own consciousness. She took a sip of her tea before setting it down on the table.

"He meant broken women, right?" she said, looking to me for answers. I nodded at her in excitement for two reasons. First, she was finally at a place to come to this awareness about herself. Second, she'd done the hard work to heal, and the results of that is enlightenment, changed behavior and perspective.

This anecdote is a prime example of the realizations we come to after a breakup, and these realizations, as painful as they may be, are paramount to healing after a difficult loss of a romantic attachment. After she said this, I continued to explain what exactly I'd meant. While her ex was toxic and a bit of a narcissist, she was, in some ways, complicit in the breakup and in what was unhealthy about their bond. This complicity is difficult to acknowledge but is no less important than the breakup itself. Your ex might've been toxic too, but simply calling them so and frolicking off into the sunset is silly and inconsequential. You too were complicit in the screaming fights, long arguments, and unhealthy behavior. Furthermore, it is paramount, and often overlooked, to consider how you ended up in this situation in the first place. While examining that role is uncomfortable and frustrating, it's pivotal to understand your shortcomings and to address those for the future.

My friend was involved in the relationship's toxicity more than she'd realized. Her brokenness enabled her partner to treat her poorly. Today, she's much happier and healthier. She realizes that her need to be loved is compulsive, and acknowledges her shortcomings. She knows that what happened wasn't her fault, but that she was involved in the relationship's downfall. I'm happy to report that she is now in a healthy, supportive, and loving relationship with a man who loves her for who she is rather than who he wants her to be.

Post-breakup grief is uncomfortable and unwanted. It feels like the convoluted loss of a part of yourself. But within this loss is an opportunity, a chance to heal. Had my friend not asked that specific question, she might've spent the rest of her adult life seeking attachments to people who only sought to exploit her insecurities. Now, with renewed information, she can completely heal from what happened, and she can improve as a result. Grief provides clarity, and for your feelings to be fruitful, you must use this clarity to improve and grow moving forward.

Reimagining Love and Relationships

With the loss of love comes a chance to grow and heal, but what happens after this process is over?

After the worst breakup of my life, I began to realize the unhealthy ways I'd engaged in relationships, but I couldn't help but think, "I just need to see her one more time." I thought that because I was healed, we could reunite and become friends. More than anything, I missed her in my life, and I lamented her positive qualities. I longed for a universe where she and I could be casual friends, going to coffee or dinner together, and chatting about our professional lives. However, for me, this idyllic universe wasn't a reality, nor did it ever become one. And for that, I'm grateful.

Social narratives emphasize the end of a romantic attachment, but this isn't always the case. You may never entirely heal from a breakup, and that is an uncomfortable reality. It's ultimately possible to be over someone but to not be over what happened and what they did to you. Other harmful social narratives portray being single as negative and paint those who choose to be single as social outcasts or pariahs. These narratives are false and misguided. Just because you're single doesn't mean you'll stay that way, and love is present in any and all stages of life.

The healing period before re-entry is not empty time. It is the most important work in this book. And like all important work, it benefits from structure. Three practices. Not requirements. Investments.

The Pattern Interruption Practice. A thirty-day commitment to noticing when your pattern fires in non-romantic contexts in friendships, in work dynamics, in family interactions. Every time it activates, apply the Reset Ritual. Practice in lower-stakes arenas so the tool is available in higher-stakes ones. The pattern does not only run in romantic relationships. It runs everywhere. The training that matters happens between relationships, not inside them.

The Blueprint Revision. A guided reflection on what the last relationship revealed about the blueprint you brought in. Not what the other person did wrong. What you brought. Use the Mask Inventory and the Attraction Pattern Audit from earlier in this book as source material. The blueprint you examine honestly before the next relationship is the one you have a chance of actually changing. The one you carry forward unexamined becomes the foundation of the next version of the same story.

The Readiness Threshold. Three behavioral capacities, not feelings, capacities that signal genuine readiness for re-entry. You can sit with discomfort without running from it or escalating it. You can speak about your last relationship without making the other person the entire explanation for what happened. You can imagine a new relationship and feel genuine curiosity rather than primarily fear or primarily hunger. These are not feelings to perform. They are states you will either inhabit or not. Honesty here is the only useful approach.

These are not rules for when you are allowed to love again. They are investments in the quality of what you build when you do.

The idea that you can find love again is a hallmark of the breakup's realization stage. The personal realizations you come to have the power to effectively shift the way you see yourself following a breakup, and act as key lessons for the relationships you engage in later. But here is what I need you to understand before you rush toward the next chapter of your romantic life.

You cannot pour from an empty cup. You've heard it before and you're hearing it again because it is true in a way that most people don't actually internalize until they've learned it the hard way. I learned it the hard way. Multiple times. I went from relationship to relationship believing that if I just found the right person, the ache would stop. What I discovered, through years of therapy, research, and honest reflection, is that the right person cannot fix what you haven't yet faced in yourself.

This is not a punishment. It is not a sentence to a life of solitude. It is an invitation. An invitation to become, before you try again, the person you would want your future partner to find.

What does that look like practically? It looks like sitting with the discomfort of being alone long enough to learn what you actually want, not what you've been taught to want, not what social media tells you is aspirational, but what genuinely feeds your spirit and aligns with your values. It looks like doing the therapeutic or coaching work to understand your pattern, whether you're an Escapist, a Rescuer, a Reactor, or a Skeptic, and taking steps to build new relational reflexes. It looks like building a life, outside of a relationship, that you don't need someone else to complete.

Because here is the truth about love that this entire book has been working toward: a healthy relationship is not two broken people fixing each other. It is two people who have done enough of their own work to stand beside each other, not lean on each other for survival, and to build something that neither of them could have built alone.

That is the relationship you deserve. That is the relationship worth waiting for. And that is the relationship that becomes possible the moment you decide that understanding yourself is not something you do before love finds you. It is the foundation on which real love is built.

Now You Know

Six months after the worst breakup of her life, Jasmine sat across from me at a coffee shop near her apartment and told me she was ready to start dating again.

I asked her how she knew.

She thought about it for a moment. Then she said, "Because I finally stopped checking his Instagram."

I smiled at that. Not because it was funny, although it was a little funny, but because I recognized it. The Instagram check is one of the last things to go. Long after the crying has stopped and the appetite has returned and the intrusive thoughts have settled from a constant roar to an occasional hum, the Instagram check persists. It is the last thread of an attachment the brain is not quite ready to release. When it stops, something real has shifted.

But I was not entirely convinced Jasmine was ready. So I asked her a different question.

"Tell me something you learned about yourself in the last six months."

She paused longer this time. The first answer, the Instagram one, had come quickly. This one required her to go somewhere she had not been asked to go in a while.

"I learned," she said slowly, "that I am a lot more afraid of being alone than I ever admitted to myself. And I think that fear is why I stayed in that relationship two years longer than I should have."

Now I was convinced. Not because she had the answer, but because she had been willing to go looking for it. Because the six months she had spent alone had not just been six months of healing. They had been six months of learning. And what she had learned about herself was going to change every relationship she entered from this point forward.

That is what this chapter is about. Not how to find love again. Not how to get back out there. Not the rules of modern dating or the algorithm for the right swipe. This chapter is about who you are now, after everything this book has walked you through, and what it means to carry that person into what comes next.

The Difference Between Ready and Healed

Let me say something clearly before we go any further, because I have watched this confusion cause real damage to real people more times than I can count.

Ready and healed are not the same thing.

Healed is a destination most of us never fully reach. Healing is not a linear process with a finish line. It is more like maintenance. Like physical fitness. You do the work, you build the strength, you develop the capacity, and then you keep doing the work because the alternative is regression. No one finishes healing and then never has to think about their patterns again. The Escapist does not do six months of therapy and wake up one morning permanently cured of the impulse to go quiet when love gets too close. The Rescuer does not read this book and suddenly stop feeling the pull to over-function in relationships. What changes is awareness. What changes is the ability to catch the pattern before it makes the decision for you.

Ready, on the other hand, is a more practical threshold. Ready means you have done enough of the work that you can bring yourself into a new relationship without the unhealed parts of you doing most of the damage. Ready means the wound has closed enough that you are not going to bleed all over the next person who gets close to you. Ready means you can sit in a room with someone who interests you and be genuinely curious about them rather than immediately running them through the filter of your worst fear, which is whether they are going to hurt you the way the last one did.

You do not have to be fully healed to be ready. But you do have to be honest about where you are.

Jasmine was ready. She had done the work. The six months had not been passive. She had been in therapy. She had sat with the discomfort of being alone. She had done the uncomfortable audit of her own role in what had gone wrong. She had learned something real about herself, that fear of being alone had been driving decisions she thought were being driven by love, and she was carrying that knowledge forward.

That is the difference between someone who is ready and someone who has simply gotten tired of being alone. Getting tired of being alone is not readiness. It is loneliness looking for a solution. And loneliness is one of the least reliable navigational tools for choosing a partner.

SIDEBAR: You will know you are ready when your primary reason for wanting a relationship is the relationship itself, not the escape from being without one.

What You Know Now That You Did Not Know Before

Let me walk you through what you actually have now, if you have done the work this book has asked of you, because I want you to understand that you are not the same person who opened this book. Or if you are, something went wrong and I want you to go back to Chapter 8 and start again.

You know your pattern.

This is the most significant thing. You know whether you are an Escapist, a Rescuer, a Reactor, or a Skeptic. You know the specific fear that drives your pattern. You know what it looks like when your pattern is activated, the specific behaviors it produces, the specific impact those behaviors have on the people who get close to you. You know the reframe, the more accurate story you can tell yourself when the pattern fires, the one that is rooted in compassion rather than shame.

This knowledge changes everything. Not because knowing your pattern makes you immune to it. As I said in Chapter 8, insight is necessary but not sufficient. But because now when the pattern fires, and it will fire, you have a name for what is happening. You can catch it before it makes a decision you will spend months recovering from. You can say to yourself: this is my Skeptic pattern testing someone who has given me no real evidence they are untrustworthy. Or: this is my Escapist pattern going quiet because vulnerability arrived and my nervous system read it as a threat. Naming it does not eliminate it. But naming it gives you a choice that you did not have before.

You know the difference between chemistry and compatibility.

You know that the roller coaster feeling, the intensity, the way someone can light you up and devastate you in equal measure, is not a sign that you have found something rare and powerful. It may be a sign that you have found someone who knows how to activate your wounds. You know that trauma bonds feel like destiny from the inside. You know that the nice person who is consistent and kind and boring in the best possible way might be offering you exactly what you have been unconsciously rejecting your entire dating life.

This does not mean you have to choose boring. It means you have to look harder at what you are calling exciting and ask yourself whether you are excited or just familiar with chaos.

You know what intimacy actually requires.

You know that it is built through time and self-disclosure and the quality of your presence with another person. You know that friendship is not a precursor to love but its foundation. You know that physical intimacy is downstream of emotional intimacy and that the gap between two people almost always begins in the emotional register long before it shows up in the physical one. You know that love, real and genuine love, is something you participate in consciously, not something that simply happens to you.

You know how to fight.

You know the difference between calling your partner out and calling your partner in. You know that conflict is not the enemy of a relationship but the doorway to what actually needs attention. You know that ultimatums are threats dressed up as boundaries and that real repair requires empathy, self-disclosure, and the willingness to see the conflict as something you and your partner are navigating together rather than something you are doing to each other.

You know what loss means.

You know that grief after a breakup is not weakness or failure. It is biology. You know that the period of time you are single after a significant loss is not a waiting room but a workshop, and that the work you do in that workshop determines what you build in the next relationship. You know that time does not heal wounds. You do.

What to Look For Now

I want to give you something practical here, because this is the chapter where practical guidance matters most. You have done the internal work. Now you are stepping back into the world. What are you actually looking for?

Not a list of qualities. I am not going to tell you to find someone kind and emotionally available and financially stable and physically attractive, because you already know those things matter and a list does not tell you how to recognize them in real time when the dopamine is doing what dopamine does.

What I want you to look for is something more specific and more useful.

Look for someone whose nervous system is compatible with yours.

This does not mean identical. It means complementary. An Escapist who has done their work can build something real with a Rescuer who has done theirs, because the Escapist's capacity for calm can steady the Rescuer's anxiety, and the Rescuer's warmth can reach the Escapist in ways that feel safe rather than threatening. But an Escapist who has not done their work and a Reactor who has not done theirs will activate each other's worst patterns in a cycle that neither of them will be able to stop.

Pay attention to how you feel in the other person's presence. Not just excited. Regulated. Does being around this person make you feel more like yourself or less? Do you feel pressure to perform or permission to be? Does their way of moving through the world create anxiety in you or settle it?

These are the questions dopamine does not let you ask in the first three months. Ask them anyway.

Let me make that guidance more specific.

The question is not which patterns are theoretically compatible. It is whether both people are doing the work that the pairing is capable of becoming.

An Escapist and a Rescuer, both working: the Escapist's capacity for calm can steady the Rescuer's anxiety without triggering the Rescuer's overfunctioning response. The Rescuer's warmth can reach the Escapist in ways that feel safe rather than demanding. The pairing works because each pattern's strength addresses the other's wound provided both people are actually doing the work. An Escapist and a Rescuer who are not working: the Rescuer gives until depleted and the Escapist retreats until the Rescuer stops reaching. The loop closes and both people leave more depleted than they arrived.

Two Reactors together, unworked: two activated nervous systems with no regulation capacity between them. The temperature is constant and the escalation mutual. There is passion, which is real, and there is damage, which is also real. Two Reactors, both working: one of the most alive relationships possible. The depth of feeling is genuine. The work required to keep it from burning everything down is equally genuine.

A Skeptic and a Rescuer, unworked: the Rescuer tries to earn trust through accumulating service and the Skeptic tests until the Rescuer has nothing left to give. The Rescuer eventually collapses or exits. The Skeptic takes it as confirmation. Both worked: the Skeptic learns that consistency is not a trap and the Rescuer learns that care does not require proving. The pairing produces depth. The path to it is not comfortable.

Two Escapists together: looks like stability. Often is. What it lacks is forward movement two people maintaining parallel distances, each waiting for the other to reach first. The relationship can function for years this way, neither person in crisis, neither person fully arrived.

The compatibility question is never which patterns can work. Almost any pairing can work with enough self-awareness and enough genuine commitment to the work. The question is which pairing you can sustain the effort of and whether you are choosing the person or choosing the familiar configuration.

At the end of this chapter, you will find the exercise on Pattern Compatibility. Use it to get an idea of how you and your partner can work together towards a healthy relationship.

Look for someone who is doing their own work.

I am not saying they need to have read this book or be in therapy or use the specific vocabulary of attachment theory. I am saying that there should be evidence, in how they talk about their past, how they take responsibility for what has not worked, how they respond when they are wrong, that this person is engaged in the process of understanding themselves and growing beyond their defaults.

Someone who has no language for their own patterns and no interest in developing any is not a person who is going to be a genuine partner in the work a real relationship requires. They are a person who is going to activate your patterns and then look at you with genuine confusion when the relationship starts to deteriorate.

You have done too much work to spend it on someone who has not started yet.

Look for friendship first.

I know you have read Chapter 11. I know you know this. I am saying it again because it is the thing most people know intellectually and ignore in practice the moment they meet someone who makes their dopamine surge.

Slow down. Let the friendship build. Let the conversations go deep before you let the physical go anywhere. Let yourself know this person in the way that creates real intimacy before you create the kind of intimacy that floods your brain with chemicals that will blind you to everything you need to see clearly.

The research is unambiguous on this. The couples who begin as friends, or who take the time to build a genuine friendship before moving into romantic territory, report higher levels of relationship satisfaction, deeper intimacy, and greater resilience during conflict than couples who moved quickly from attraction to commitment. This is not a rule. It is not a mandate. It is simply what the data shows, and the data is telling you something worth listening to.

The Friends-First Framework in Practice

In Chapter 11 we talked about the friends-first framework as a theoretical foundation for romantic relationships. I want to make it practical now, for the specific moment you are in, which is the moment of re-entry.

What does building friendship first actually look like when you are an adult with a full life and a limited tolerance for ambiguity and a pattern that either rushes toward people or retreats from them?

It looks like asking better questions earlier. Not what do you do for work, but what made you choose that work. Not where did you grow up, but what did growing up there teach you about the world. Not what are you looking for in a relationship, but what has a relationship cost you that you did not expect to pay.

It looks like spending time together in contexts that are not dates. Not dinner and drinks, where the romantic frame is doing all the work and you are both performing slightly elevated versions of yourselves. Doing something together. Going somewhere. Meeting each other's people. Seeing how they move through the world when the pressure of impressing you is not the primary organizing force of the evening.

It looks like paying attention to the small things before the large ones claim all your attention. How do they treat people who serve them? What do they do when something goes wrong that they did not cause? What is their relationship with accountability? How do they talk about the people who have hurt them? These things are visible early if you are looking for them. Most of us are not looking for them because we are too busy managing our own presentation and hoping they like us.

Look for them. They will tell you more about who this person is than anything they say on purpose.

The Relationship You Are Building With Yourself

I want to close this chapter with something that might be the most important thing in it, and it is not about finding a partner.

The healthiest relationships I have ever witnessed, in my practice and in my personal life, share one quality that I have not seen replicated in the unhealthy ones. Both people in those relationships have a genuine, sustaining relationship with themselves. They have lives outside the relationship that feed them. They have a sense of who they are that does not require the relationship to define it. They bring themselves into the partnership rather than looking to the partnership to create a self they can inhabit.

This is the work that never stops. Not because you are broken but because you are alive and changing and the person you are at thirty-four is not the person you will be at forty-one, and the person you are at forty-one deserves the same quality of self-examination and self-compassion you brought to this process.

The Re/Model framework, the one this book has been building chapter by chapter, is not a program you complete. It is a practice you maintain. You understand your pattern and you keep watching for it. You understand the difference between chemistry and compatibility and you keep applying that understanding even when dopamine is arguing with you. You understand what intimacy requires and you keep investing in it even when life makes it inconvenient. You understand how to fight and you keep choosing to fight well even when your worst impulses are pushing you toward your worst habits.

This is what it means to begin again. Not to start over from zero. To start forward from everything you now know.

Jasmine went back to dating about two months after our coffee shop conversation. She did it slowly and with intention. She stopped two relationships early when she recognized patterns in herself that she was not yet ready to bring to another person. She stayed in one that surprised her with its gentleness and its steadiness and its complete absence of the chaos she had spent years mistaking for passion.

The last time I spoke with her, she used a phrase that I have not been able to stop thinking about since.

She said, "I think for the first time in my life, I am in a relationship and I still feel like myself."

That is it. That is the whole thing. That is what all of this work is for.

Not the ring. Not the wedding. Not the Instagram post that announces to the world that you are loved. The quiet, private, sustaining experience of being in a relationship and still feeling like yourself.

That is available to you. It is not a fantasy. It is not reserved for people who were dealt a better hand or who did not carry the wounds you carried. It is available to anyone willing to do the work of understanding who they are and what they are bringing to love.

The Framework works, if you work it

Phase 1 asked you to find it. The pattern. The wound underneath it. The ego that runs it when you are activated. The mask that hides it in the beginning and always, always comes off. Remove the Gridlock. Section II.

Phase 2 asked you to rebuild what the pattern damaged. The foundation of friendship before romance. The language of conflict that moves toward truth. The intimacy rebuilt deliberately rather than rekindled from a past that neither of you can return to. Recalibrate the Connection. Section III.

Phase 3 asked you to earn what comes next by moving through what came before. To grieve completely enough that the grief does not follow you into the next chapter. To step forward with new relational reflexes rather than the inherited ones that brought you to this book in the first place. Accelerate the Results. Section IV.

You have done all three. Not perfectly. Not without resistance. But you moved through it. And moving through something, even imperfectly, is how the work gets done.

Now go build a relationship with it.

Exercise: The Pattern Compatibility Map
https://go.carloshines.com/book/pattern-compatibility
or Scan the QR Code below

Conclusion

I want to tell you something I don't say enough, to the people who sit across from me in coaching sessions, to the audiences I stand in front of around the world, and to the readers who find this book at exactly the right moment in their lives.

You are not the problem.

Your patterns are not evidence of a fundamental defect. Your failed relationships are not proof that you are unlovable. Your history of choosing wrong, staying too long, leaving too fast, or loving too hard does not disqualify you from the kind of relationship you actually want. It qualifies you. It means you've been trying. It means love matters enough to you that you kept going back to it even when it kept costing you something.

But trying harder in the same direction is not the same as moving forward. And this book, all of it, the science and the stories and the frameworks and the hard truths, has been an attempt to help you change the direction, not the effort.

Let me bring you back to where we started.

In the very first chapter of this book, I told you that we are not taught how to have healthy relationships. We absorb what we see. We internalize what we're shown. We mistake what's familiar for what's right. And then we go out into the world and build relationships from those inherited blueprints, wondering why they keep falling apart in the same places, in the same ways, with different people wearing different faces.

What I hope you understand now, having traveled through every chapter of this book, is that this was never your fault. But it is your responsibility.

There is a distinction there that matters enormously. Fault looks backward. It assigns blame and stops there. Responsibility looks forward. It says: now that I know, what do I do with the knowing?

Here is what I want you to do with the knowing.

I want you to think about the pattern you recognized in yourself back in Chapter 8. Maybe you saw yourself in the Escapist, the one who goes quiet when love gets too close, who has mastered the art of disappearing before anyone can leave first. Maybe you recognized the Rescuer, the one who gives and gives until there is nothing left, who has confused exhaustion with devotion and self-abandonment with love. Maybe it was the Reactor, the one who feels everything at full volume, who learned long ago that the only way to be heard was to be loud. Or maybe it was the Skeptic, the one who wants love more than they will admit but has been burned enough times that wanting it feels dangerous.

Whichever pattern you recognized, I want you to understand that pattern did not appear out of nowhere. It was built, carefully and necessarily, in response to an environment that required it. It kept you safe when safety was not guaranteed. It helped you survive rooms and relationships and childhoods that were not designed for your thriving.

But survival strategies have a shelf life. And the one you have been carrying, the one that served you so well for so long, is likely the same one that is standing between you and the love you say you want.

This is not a reason for shame. It is a reason for awareness. And awareness, as I told you in that chapter, is the beginning. It is not the finish line.

I want you to think about what we learned about the hidden curriculum of relationships, about the ways we absorb what is never spoken, the family dynamics that showed us what love looks like before we had words for what we were watching, the media that sold us an illusion and called it aspiration, the cultural scripts that told us who was supposed to want what and who was supposed to provide it.

None of us chose our first classrooms. None of us got to raise our hand and say, "Excuse me, I'd like a different example." We got what we got, and we made meaning from it the best we could.

But now you have new material. Now you have a language for what you were watching. Now you can ask the question that titles the first chapter of this book, not as an accusation, but as an inquiry. Who taught you that? And more importantly: is what they taught you still serving you?

I want you to think about the difference between chemistry and compatibility, about the way a trauma bond can feel like destiny, about how we mistake intensity for depth and shared pain for connection. I want you to carry forward the understanding that love is not something that happens to you. It is something you participate in. Consciously, deliberately, and with full knowledge of what you are bringing to it and what you are asking the other person to hold.

This means doing the work before you need to. Not waiting until the relationship is already in free fall to wonder why the foundation is crumbling. Not waiting until you are sitting across from a coach or a therapist in crisis to ask the questions this book has been asking you all along.

The oxygen mask goes on you, first. Always.

I want you to think about what you now know about conflict, about how it is not the enemy of your relationship but the doorway to the parts of it that most need your attention. About how calling your partner in is an act of love that calling them out will never be. About how the couples who last are not the ones who never fight, but the ones who fight and repair, fight and repair, each time coming back to the table with a little more understanding of the person across from them.

I want you to think about what you now know about breakups, about how grief is not weakness but biology, about how the period of time you are single is not a waiting room but a workshop. About how the relationship you are building right now, with yourself, is the most important relationship in this book.

Here is what I know after years of research, years of working with clients, years of sitting with people in their pain and their confusion and their hope: the people who build the healthiest relationships are not the people who were dealt the best hands. They are the people who were willing to look honestly at the hand they were dealt, understand how it shaped them, and make a conscious decision to play it differently going forward.

That is all this book has ever asked of you.

Not perfection. Not an immediate transformation. Not the performance of a healed person. Just honesty. Just the willingness to look at yourself with the same compassion you would offer someone you love, and to say: here is who I am, here is where I came from, here is what I am still working on, and here is who I am committed to becoming.

That commitment is the beginning of every healthy relationship. Not the ring. Not the wedding. Not the moment someone swipes right or makes eye contact across a crowded room. The commitment to yourself, made in private, to stop repeating what you were taught and start building what you actually want.

I told you in the Introduction that this book is not about communication. I told you that we don't need another book about communication. We need a framework that helps us see our own patterns clearly and change them.

I hope this book has been that framework for you.

I hope you have seen yourself in these pages, not in a way that shamed you, but in a way that named something you had been feeling but couldn't quite articulate. I hope the stories, Callie and Ryan, Mia and Drew, Imani and Alexia, Ross and David, Marcus and Diane, Ashley and Jose, felt true to something you have lived or witnessed. I hope the science gave you permission to stop blaming yourself for responses that were never in your control to begin with. And I hope the tools gave you something concrete to carry out of these pages and into your actual life.

This is the work. It is not glamorous. It does not have a highlight reel. It happens in the quiet moments when you choose to respond instead of react, when you choose to stay in the conversation instead of going silent, when you choose to ask for what you need instead of resenting someone for not reading your mind.

It happens when you put down the bag of bricks you have been carrying from relationship to relationship and decide that you are not going to haul them into the next one.

It happens when you stop asking your partner to fill the gaps your parents left, and start filling some of those gaps yourself.

It happens when you realize that healthy love does not feel like chaos. It does not feel like a roller coaster. It does not feel like trying to hold water in your hands. It feels, in the best moments, like finally being in a room where the temperature is right. Like being known, and not being destroyed by the knowing.

That love exists. I have seen it. I have helped people build it. And I believe, fully and without reservation, that it is available to you.

But it starts here. With this. With the willingness to ask who taught you that, and to decide, with intention and courage and the full weight of everything you now know, to teach yourself something better.

Begin again.

Continue the Work

This book gave you the framework. What comes next is the work.

The Re/Model framework™ was built for exactly what you're standing at right now: the moment after the awareness, when you know what your pattern is and you understand where it came from, but you still have to figure out what to do with it in real time, in real relationships, under real pressure.

That is where most self-help stops. And where Re/Model begins.

Start with the assessment. If you haven't taken the Re/Model Pattern Assessment yet, do it before you do anything else. It identifies your dominant relationship pattern, the specific fear architecture underneath it, and the ways it is showing up in your life right now. It takes five minutes. It will give you a level of clarity about yourself that most people spend years in therapy trying to reach. **www.carloshines.com/quiz**

Go deeper with the framework. The Re/Model Masterclass is a live virtual and offered in person event that deep dives into the full framework, covering the four patterns in detail, the relational literacy skills that interrupt them, and the specific tools for rebuilding how you show up in love. It is the most direct path from knowing your pattern to changing it.

Work alongside others. The Re/Model Cohort brings together a small group of people doing this work at the same time, with structured curriculum, real-time application, and direct access to me throughout the process. If you learn better in community and with accountability, this is where you belong.

Work with me directly. A limited number of private coaching engagements are available each quarter for individuals who are ready to do this work at the highest level of depth and support. If that is you, the information is at **www.carloshines.com/framework**.

Whatever your next step is, take it. The awareness you built inside this book is only as valuable as what you do with it.

Bibliography

Ahn, Y. "Yearning for Affection: Traumatic Bonding Between Korean 'Comfort Women' and Japanese Soldiers During World War II." *European Journal of Women's Studies* 26, no. 4 (2018): 360–374.

Almakias, S., and A. Weiss. "Ultimatum Game Behavior in Light of Attachment Theory." *Journal of Economic Psychology* 33, no. 3 (2012): 515–526.

Alonso-Ferres, M., I. Martínez, J. J. Navarro-Pérez, and F. Megías-Lizancos. "Avoidant Attachment, Withdrawal-Aggression Conflict Pattern, and Relationship Satisfaction." *Frontiers in Psychology* 12 (2022): 794942.

Alonso-Ferres, M., I. Valor-Segura, and F. Expósito. "Couple Conflict-Facing Responses from a Gender Perspective." *Psychosocial Intervention* 28, no. 3 (2019): 147–156.

Arikewuyo, A. O., T. T. Lasisi, S. S. Abdulbaqi, A. I. Omoloso, and H. O. Arikewuyo. "Evaluating the Use of Social Media in Escalating Conflicts in Romantic Relationships." *Journal of Public Affairs* 22, no. 1 (2020).

Aušraitė, M., and K. Žardeckaitė-Matulaitienė. "The Relationship Between Irrational Relationship Beliefs and Conflict Resolution Strategies in Young Adulthood." *International Journal of Psychology: A Biopsychosocial Approach* 23 (2019): 77–93.

Bastian, B., J. Jetten, and L. J. Ferris. "Pain as Social Glue." *Psychological*

Science 25, no. 11 (2014): 2079–2085.

Benecke, A., Y. Inbar, and T. Shomrat. "From Emotional Abuse to a Fear of Intimacy." *International Journal of Environmental Research and Public Health* 21, no. 12 (2024): 1679.

Chapman, Gary. *The 5 Love Languages: The Secret to Love That Lasts.* Chicago: Northfield Publishing, 2015.

Cohen, M. "An Exploratory Study of Individuals in Non-Traditional, Alternative Relationships." *Sexuality & Culture* 20, no. 2 (2015): 295–315.

Costos, D. "Gender Role Identity from an Ego Developmental Perspective." *Sex Roles* 22 (1990): 723–741.

Davis, D. "How the Brain Rewires as We Grieve." *Psychology Today*, 2023.

Dewitte, M., J. van Lankveld, S. Vandenberghe, and T. Loeys. "Exploring the Link Between Daily Relationship Quality, Sexual Desire, and Sexual Activity in Couples." *Archives of Sexual Behavior* 47, no. 6 (2018): 1675–1686.

Dixon, S. "Daily Time Spent on Social Networking by Internet Users Worldwide." *Statista*, 2022.

Downey, G., and S. I. Feldman. "Implications of Rejection Sensitivity for Intimate Relationships." *Journal of Personality and Social Psychology* 70, no. 6 (1996): 1327–1343.

Dutton, D. G. "Anger in Intimate Relationships." In *Anger, Aggression, and Interventions for Interpersonal Violence.* Lawrence Erlbaum Associates, 2007.

Edwards, S. "Love and the Brain." *Harvard*, 2015.

Eickmeyer, K., P. Hemez, W. Manning, S. Brown, and K. Benjamin Guzzo. *Trends in Relationship Formation and Stability in the United States*. 2020.

Ellison, N., R. Heino, and J. Gibbs. "Managing Impressions Online." *Journal of Computer-Mediated Communication* 11, no. 2 (2006): 415–441.

Field, T. "Romantic Breakups, Heartbreak and Bereavement." *Psychology* 2, no. 4 (2011): 382–387.

Fletcher, G., J. Simpson, and A. Boyes. "Accuracy and Bias of Judgments in Romantic Relationships." *Current Directions in Psychological Science* 24, no. 4 (2015): 292–297.

Forgas, J. P., and J. Fitness. *Social Relationships: Cognitive, Affective and Motivational Processes*. Psychology Press, 2015.

Gibson, T. G. "If You Want the Milk, Buy the Cow." Electronic Theses and Dissertations, 2020.

Gilbert, S. P., and S. K. Sifers. "Bouncing Back from a Breakup." *Journal of College Student Psychotherapy* 25, no. 4 (2011): 295–310.

Gottman, J. M., J. Driver, and A. Tabares. "Repair During Marital Conflict in Newlyweds." *Journal of Family Psychotherapy* 26, no. 2 (2015): 85–108.

Gottman, John M., and Nan Silver. *The Seven Principles for Making Marriage Work*. New York: Crown Publishing, 1999.

Grote, N. K., and I. H. Frieze. "The Measurement of Friendship-Based Love in Intimate Relationships." *Personal Relationships* 1, no. 3 (1994): 275–300.

Hall, J. A. "How Many Hours Does It Take to Make a Friend?" *Journal of Social and Personal Relationships* 36, no. 4 (2018): 1278–1296.

Hernández Yumar, A., et al. "Emotional Flooding in Couple Relationships." IntechOpen, 2024.

Holmes, B. M., and K. R. Johnson. "Adult Attachment and Romantic Partner Preference." *Journal of Social and Personal Relationships* 26 (2009): 833–852.

Ickes, W. "Traditional Gender Roles." *Journal of Social Issues* 49, no. 3 (1993): 71–85.

Joel, S., G. MacDonald, and E. Page-Gould. "Wanting to Stay and Wanting to Go." *Social Psychological and Personality Science* 9, no. 6 (2017): 631–644.

Laurenceau, J.-P., L. F. Barrett, and P. R. Pietromonaco. "Intimacy as an Interpersonal Process." *Journal of Personality and Social Psychology* 74, no. 5 (1998): 1238–1251.

LaMotte, S. "Are You in Love or Just High on Chemicals in Your Brain?" *CNN*, 2020.

Long, D. M. "Impression Management." *Oxford Research Encyclopedia of Psychology*, 2021.

Moors, A. C., J. L. Matsick, and H. A. Schechinger. "Unique and Shared Relationship Benefits." *European Psychologist* 22, no. 1 (2017): 55–71.

New International Bible. *The NIV Bible*. 2011.

Orzek, T., and A. Rokach. "Relationship Trauma." *International Journal of Psychology and Counselling* 3, no. 3 (2011): 55–61.

Perilloux, C., and D. M. Buss. "Breaking Up Romantic Relationships." *Evolutionary Psychology* 6, no. 1 (2008).

Prager, K. J., et al. "Withdrawal, Attachment Security, and Recovery from Conflict." *Journal of Social and Personal Relationships* 36, no. 2 (2019): 573–598.

Raypole, C. "How to Recognize and Heal from Relationship PTSD." *Healthline*, 2021.

Reimer, J. E., and A. R. Estrada. "College Students' Grief Over a Breakup." *Journal of Loss and Trauma* (2020).

Reyome, N. D., K. S. Ward, and K. Witkiewitz. "Psychosocial Variables as Mediators." *Journal of Aggression, Maltreatment & Trauma* 19, no. 2 (2010): 159–179.

Rokach, A., and D. VanderVoort. "Posttraumatic Relationship Syndrome." *Journal of Social Distress and the Homeless* 16, no. 1 (2007): 22–48.

Sabik, N. J., J. Falat, and J. Magagnos. "When Self-Worth Depends on Social Media Feedback." *Sex Roles* 82 (2019).

Schneiderman, I., et al. "Oxytocin During the Initial Stages of Romantic Attachment." *Psychoneuroendocrinology* 37, no. 8 (2012): 1277–1285.

Smith, M. B. "'The Ego Ideal of the Good Camper.'" *Environmental History* 11, no. 1 (2006): 70–101.

Sprecher, S., and S. Metts. "Romantic Beliefs." *Journal of Social and Personal Relationships* 16, no. 6 (1999): 834–851.

Sternberg, R. J. "A Triangular Theory of Love." *Psychological Review* 93, no. 2 (1986): 119–135.

Stephenson, G. R. "Cultural Acquisition of a Specific Learned Response." In

Progress in Primatology. Stuttgart: Fischer, 1967.

Stinson, D. A., J. J. Cameron, and L. B. Hoplock. "The Friends-to-Lovers Pathway to Romance." *Social Psychological and Personality Science* 12, no. 2 (2021).

Thomas, K. W. Thomas-kilmann conflict mode. *TKI Profile and Interpretive Report,* 1(11).

Utz, S., and C. J. Beukeboom. "The Role of Social Network Sites in Romantic Relationships." *Journal of Computer-Mediated Communication* 16, no. 4 (2011): 511–527.

Van Lankveld, J., et al. "The Associations of Intimacy and Sexuality in Daily Life." *Journal of Social and Personal Relationships* 35, no. 4 (2018): 557–576.

Wang, W., K. Zhou, Z. Yu, and J. Li. "The Cost of Impression Management to Life Satisfaction." *Psychology Research and Behavior Management* 13 (2020): 407–417.

Yildiz, B. "Attachment, Growth Fear and Conflict Resolution." *International Journal of Psychology and Educational Studies* 10, no. 2 (2023): 453–462.

About the Author

Dr. Carlos Hines is a trauma and relational psychology expert, researcher, and the founder of the Re/Model framework, a root-cause approach to understanding and transforming relational dysfunction. His work is grounded in original relational literacy research conducted in New York City, and draws on more than a decade of work at the intersection of trauma, identity, and human connection.

Dr. Hines works with private clients, leads cohort-based programs, and speaks to audiences navigating the deeper patterns that shape how they relate to others and to themselves. His approach is methodical in its precision and human in its delivery. He believes that relational change is not a matter of motivation. It is a matter of doing the work.

You can connect with me on:

 https://www.carloshines.com